THE Inner VOICE

THE Inner VOICE

RAHSAAN AKI TAYLOR

J. KENKADE PUBLISHING ™

A division of J. Kenkade Enterprises, LLC

The Inner Voice
Copyright © 2017 by Rahsaan Aki Taylor

J. Kenkade Publishing
6104 Forbing Rd
Little Rock, AR 72209
www.jkenkade.com
Facebook.com/JKenkade

J. Kenkade Publishing is an imprint of
J. Kenkade Enterprises, LLC.
The J. Kenkade Publishing name and logo
are trademarks of J. Kenkade Enterprises, LLC.

Printed in the United States of America
ISBN 978-1-944486-61-7

This book is dedicated to my beautiful daughter, Mariyah K. Taylor. You will forever be my intelligent princess. Happy Birthday Sweetie!

Table of Contents

Acknowledgments

I would like to give a high praise to the most awesome God. Jehovah Jireh, you made all things possible for me. I want to thank my mother for being there for me when no one else was. You are a true soldier. Truth be told, you are stronger than me! (Ssshh don't tell anyone that).

I would like to thank all of my siblings starting with my baby sister Tichina Taylor. You are my strength, my heart, and sometimes I feel as if you are my very own child.

Shekila Moore Jones, you are the standup type— the kind that holds me up when I'm down. I feel like we can go against the world because I know you're going to ride until the wheels fall off, and if the wheels fall off, you're going to ride with me on rims, hubcaps, rotors, and frames!

Nioka Taylor Smith, what can I say? I guess as time moves on and we get older, we grow a little distant. Yet, nothing shall remove my love for you and I know that I am in your heart.

Keith Moore, my brilliant brother, I love you. I'm still waiting on a permanent and divine change. My prayers are with you. Never give up or think that it is too late. Have you ever heard of miracles? We are miracles!

Ziyaan Taylor, my mighty son in all of his ways. Please choose the righteous road to go down. Life is full of choices, almost like multiple choice exams at school. Avoid errors.

Mariyah Keona Taylor, you are forever daddy's little princess. Never settle for less or let anyone devalue you. You are the head and not the tail!

Lawrence Morris (DJ), I love you boy! Keep your head up and always make wise decisions. Remember you are setting an example for your brother and sisters.

My wonderful grandmother, my cousins Sunshine, Milton, Shamika, Kentrell, and Tonya thanks for keeping in touch with me regardless of my conditions. Aunt Virgina and Aunt Lean, I haven't forgotten what you have done for me in the beginning.

To Tamara Arthurs, my fans, family, and friends, lets continue to support and encourage one another. You all hold a special place in my heart.

Big shout to everyone that is connected to me

through Facebook. You were the first ones to receive a piece of me. I thank you all!

Introduction

This book contains matters and reasoning that has been controversial throughout the world for many generations. Unfortunately, I am not here to settle disputes or stir up debates amongst civilized citizens. I know how easily sensitivity is provoked subconsciously. However, I am ordained to shed a light and bring an awakening to certain dormant spectacles. Most of the time when I speak, I do not only speak to hearers and readers, but sometimes I speak to myself. I teach others, while also teaching myself. I have studied line upon line and percept upon percept. I do not consider myself to be omniscient, omnipresent, overly sagacious, or omnipotent. I am suspected to make mistakes. Yet, I was called to write this book because I see, understand, and have knowledge of particular areas where the average person lacks. A lot of people are not going to agree with what I have written in the contents of this book. Many will dislike me for the incisiveness of my linguistics. But it's okay. They hate Jesus Christ, Elijah Muhammed, Buddha, and other great men till this day. I am not trying to be friendly but if I become a friend of the family, then I welcome you. I am not trying to save the world; that is an impossible task to ponder. My goal is to reach at least one soul. I want to capture the attention and pray that whoever you are, you will hold on for dear life to what I have taught. In result, you will teach another, and that person will teach the next and so on.

Although, you will probably hate me for the incisive truth that I bring to the table, society has debilitated the minds of this modern world. Therefore, some people are accustoming to passiveness, pacifying, and people telling them what they want to hear. Some even believe that they are not supposed to be corrected. This book will exhort, rebuke, and persuade. It will literally cut the hearts of most because of the overly aggressive language. I must admit that I have a way with words. Disagreeing with me is okay. However, in no shape, form, or fashion will I debate. I live by the motto, *it's alright if we agree to disagree.* I am not here to make you feel good! Neither, do I consider myself "holier than thou".

Chapter 1

GOD

Is there really such a thing as a God? If so, how do you know? Have you seen him? Why do we call God a man? What does he look like?

I remember once being in a meeting with an atheist. Being the inquisitive person that I am, I just had to ask, "Why don't you believe in God?" He turned to face me with an inflammatory expression and waved his hand dismissively. Then he answered, "Man I just don't." If you know anything about me then you know that I was not going to let that go. So, I responded to him saying, "Well, how do you think you were born?" Sarcastically he said, "From my momma." I asked, "Who do you think made your momma and daddy?" Of course, his response was exactly what I had expected it to be. He berated, "From their momma and daddy?"

I saw right then and there that this conversation was not going anywhere. So, I just asked him the grand question. With all the enthusiasm in the world, I asked the question like I was at a carnival trying to get someone to win a consultation prize. I asked him, "**Who do you think created the first human being that was ever created?!**" Unfortunately, this guy had a relatively peculiar reply. He chided, "I don't know, but I guess chromosomes, molecules, and atoms." He went on to imply, "Some say people come from monkeys and apes." I looked at him like he was ludicrous. I inquired, "Who do you think made the atoms, molecules, and chromosomes then?" He couldn't respond right away. I gave him a moment to anticipate his next avenue. After contemplating for a while, he did just that. "You don't have anything to say about the monkeys and apes?!" I shook my head then I walked away. I could no longer participate in this insidious conversation. After his last response, he confirmed my favorite motto that I came up with. *The only thing worse than not thinking at all, is thinking too much.*

Some people go in overdrive with their thoughts. Their discernment is based upon perceptibility. Have you ever seen someone that just moves too fast? They often stumble or miss out on something that is valuable. If they would just slow down and take their time, every move would be calculated adequately and leave less room for errors. It is the same way with thoughts. Instead of having images created to fit your arbitrary, take the time out to study, research, and feel what's beyond carnality. Don't run along with the first thing that seems factual. Your conception can become misconception.

A lot of people are dormant because of what scientist say. They proclaim that the Bible and the Quran are like a fairy tale. They insist that a professor's hypothesis deviates their brain from fathoming that a God exists. A young lady once told me that she did not believe in The Most High because man had a theory for every creation. I never informed her back then, but young lady, if you are reading this book, don't let science control your thinking ability.

It is well known that atoms make up the world around us including the following: whatever goes into a building, insects, and even dirt. Everything is made up of tiny atoms and is broken down into trillions of protons, neutrons, and electrons. Atoms make up a person's weight. In a person who weighs 149 lbs. and 15 oz. are protons, neutrons, and only 1 ounce are electrons. Believe it or not, there would be no such thing as matter if there were not any atoms. Everything we can see touch, taste, smell, even the things that we hear are made up of atoms. Atoms can even spin at a certain degree to create noise.

Despite all the scientific facts, it still does not refute the obvious. Whoever created the atoms, molecules, and chromosomes is still unknown to science. Surely, the particles are not an entity. They did not create themselves! There are a lot of things experts do not have a theory for. Then again, even if scientists did have a theory for everything, who is to say that their theory is accurate? A theory does not necessarily mean it is correct. A theory is only an educated guess.

According to Webster Dictionary, a theory means assumption or speculation (Theory).

People, there is a God! If not, then who created the moon and told it to come out at its rightful time? Who created the sun and the planets that orbit around it? What man can travel to space and live comfortably forever? Who gave the first breathe of life? What about the equinox? It's a line that divides the night from day. Who put the water, grass, and air on earth? How do the seasons know when to come? Who keeps the clouds leveled? Who told earth not to fall off its axes?

Today, people clutter their mind trying to figure out what's real. My definition of real may not be what is real to you, and your meaning may not be what is real to me. So, what is real? Is it only what you can see or feel? Does it not exist if you can't? Surely, you can't see the wind but it's there. The breath in your body is not visible but it is present. Everything is not for you to understand. Some knowledge exceeds your capacity to learn. Scales have been placed on your eyes. Your ears have been clogged with more than wax. The true teacher's mouths have been muffled and hearts no longer flow with unconditional love.

The reason for this is because the greatest treasure lies between two temples. Thousands have searched for these temples, yet they have not uncovered its natural identity. Once you construe this riddle, then your life will change.

Do you really have to see something all the time to believe in it? Most people do. Even after they see it or the effects of it, they will later need reassurance. Doubt is easier to capture than faith. Most people would rather relax than to struggle and exhaust their remedies whether it is spiritually, mentally, physically, or emotionally.

After dealing with agnostics, my mind grew weary on how to ingratiate, so I drew up a census during an intervention. I asked, how do you know that the Creator is real? My siblings were the first to respond. They answered, "Because he's in my soul. He lives within me. He is a part of me that is always with me. You should feel to know he's real. You don't hear the wind blowing until you have tuned into it." When you remove all other distractions, your senses become aware and you can hear him. However, he has been there all along. Your senses were just not tuned in. To sum it up, my mother wrote a nine-page letter.

She said, "There is no explanation for God because he is God. This is why you must believe and have faith. He is not seen or heard with normal senses. He is felt, seen, and heard with spiritual senses." A close friend sent a text to me saying, "That's a hard one." An acquaintance wrote, "He does wonderful things. He's the reason I am alive, and you are alive." Another friend said, "Not believing in God is like believing in electricity and not believing in the current."

Everybody else spoke from personal experience. With all that said and done, God cannot be understood by anyone *for you*. You must conclude that you will be held accountable for your own soul.

If you did not believe that there was a God and there was one, your unbelief could cause you to lose proper preparations for eternity. So, you may live ignoring the existent of such a higher being. Maybe the revelation of the true rapture will come, but you are denied the privilege to enter the pearly gates.

I have a question that I would love for you to reiterate for the rest of your life. Would it be better for you to go through life preparing to be with God and find out that there is not one? Or to go through life living like there was not a God and find out that there is one? Now before you answer this question, remember that you were warned.

One thing about opinions is that you can't argue with opinions. The only thing that you can do with opinions is to point out the weaknesses in them. Some people are stuck on objects that distract them from looking at the big picture. They are drawn away from the truth by deception or miscellaneous things and unaware that *false evidence appears real*. So, the things that they see are not really the things that they are.

Romans 11:8
"God hath given them the spirit
of slumber, eyes that they should
not see, and ears they should not hear."

It is not for everyone to know the way and the will of God. The word says, "Seek ye first the kingdom of heaven then everything else will be added unto you." (Mathew 6: 33) If you lack understanding then ask for it. Some people are too stubborn, brain washed, or stuck in their ways to ask for an understanding of the Most High.

The Almighty wants to have a relationship with us. If you don't want to believe, then you can't receive clairvoyance or omniscience. Get to know the Holiest of Holy for yourself. If you search deep down into your inner being you will discover the supernatural that has been there all the time. It's that inner peace that we have always felt oblige to fill that void. Don't get mislead by fables like the "monkey" story. Of course, animals have been here since the beginning of time.

Men tame animals. Animals don't tame men.

Our intelligence level is much more eminent than that of an inferior species. So, the next time that someone suspects that men came from monkeys, ask them, "Where his tail is at?" Monkeys do have tails, right? Or when someone says that atoms, molecules, or chromosomes started the first human race, ask them who fed, sheltered, and clothed the first infant child that was ever created? Who raised this child and taught him how to function? Surely the atoms and chromosomes didn't! So, my question to you is who created man?

Even in insurance policies there is a thing called an "Act of God." Why? Some things are unexplainable. That is why the scriptures instruct us to walk by faith and not by sight. Now, what is faith?

Hebrews 11:1
"Now faith is the substance of
things hoped for, and the evidence
of things not seen."

If you don't have the hope or belief—even though the evidence may be in front of you or comes later, you will never be ready to accept it.

I dug deeper into this thing called *faith*. As stated by Webster Dictionary, faith is defined as-confident belief, trust, religious conviction loyalty, and allegiance(Faith). Yet, the thing that stuck out the most to me was *conviction*. I am convinced that even though I can't put my finger on God, I have enough belief to trust Him with my life. The outcome of my circumstances and problems are evidence if His existence, even though I can't see Him with my natural eye.

God is like energy. Energy can't be fully explained on how it came about. All that we know is that energy cannot be destroyed. It can only be transformed into another element.

Chapter 2

Heaven

Heaven is not a fairytale. It is very real.

Isaiah 55:8-9

"For my thoughts are not your thoughts,

neither are your ways my ways,

sayeth the Lord. For as the heavens

are higher than the earth,

so are my ways higher than your ways,

and my thoughts than your thoughts."

There's a group of people, particularly non-believers in the nation of Islam that do not believe that there is a heaven. They say that when you're dead, it is over; there is no afterlife. It is sad but true that a higher power has closed their mind to the point that they are incapable of using the full percentage of their brain.

People can't understand what they don't know. Just think about it. If you would have never known there was such a thing called "planet earth", would you believe that there could be a thing like land or water? Would you be in doubt because you never saw it?

Who is there to put a limitation on God? Who can undermine the creator? He said, "Let there be light" and there was light (Genesis 1: 3). Not only did He create the non-existent light, but Jehovah also divided the light from the darkness. How powerful is that?

A wise man once told me that if you are searching for the truth, then first find a lie. If you find a lie then a lie is not the truth. Ironically, a lot of people were informed to only believe half of the bible. They have been mentally seared with a hot iron to the point where they only study the Old Testament. Even though the New Testament comes after the Old Testament, they say that the New Testament is irrelevant. Revelation and the resurrection are incoherent to their understanding.

Today I would like to enlighten these people that have been persuaded from the truth, distracted, and blindsided from what's in front of them. If you pay attention to the very first verse of Genesis, it tells you in the beginning God created heaven and earth. How could you disregard the first words that were written in the Holy Bible? Not to mention that it's the Old Testament. Have you ever thought that your dogma could be insufficient, or your teacher could have been misled somewhere down the line?

Most believe that pies don't fall from the sky anymore, or should I say "bread", as it really states in the scripture (Exodus 16:4). I was in a classification meeting one day because of a discipline that I was served. However, the board was considering whether they should restore me back to my recent position. Now let me inform you that this is a stern committee and punishment is their first nature. Sometimes, during the phase of them reciting my violations, they would ask me if I had anything to say. I said one line and I quote, "I don't even know why I am up here because I have gotten a disciplinary in four years."

After I made that statement, the major took over the floor for me and spoke in my favor. I was shocked. These people loved to hand out unusual punishment, but for some reason it was like a chain reaction. I felt a spirit move. The entire board began to work into my grace. Now I know this may not mean much to you, but if you knew what I knew, or been where I've been, you would know that after years and many struggles to get to the comfortable position where I was, it would have been a total breakdown to lose it.

What I'm trying to say is that pies and bread fall from the heavens in many different shapes, forms, and fashions. What's meant for me may not be what's meant for you. Your needs and desires are totally different from mine (Exodus 16:11-18). Some people confuse what manna really is. During the Israelites journey through the wilderness, they needed food to be provided to them to fill their belly. Just so happen that as they were a migrating flock of quails. While they cried out for food, God said that he was going to give them meat to eat. Take note that this is the first time that it was recorded that man ate flesh (Exodus 16:12). When the quails landed on the ground, they surrounded the camp. In the morning, dew was turned into a tasty snack. (Exodus 16:13-15)

To all those that believe heaven is on earth, I suppose that earth is really not earth to you; it's heaven. This is the same heaven that's mentioned several times in the Old Testament that some were taught to believe. Please take the time to read the scriptures listed below:

Deuteronomy 26:15
I Chronicles 16:26
II Chronicles 2:12
I Kings 8:30-49
Nehemiah 9:6
Job 9:8; 14:2
Isaiah 65:17; 66:22; 34:4
Psalms 102: 23-26

These scriptures have been there all along. So, what is your truth for you to believe in the Old Testament and not believe in heaven? There's a worldly saying today that says, "I want my cake and eat it too" and "I want my piece of the pie". However, I don't know what your pie or cake may be referring to. When that major spoke up for me in the meeting, that was all the pie I needed. When someone just hands me a gift, who is there to say that gift didn't come from heaven? A heavenly blessing may be sent down from above through someone else!

Your joy may not be my joy. My pain is not your pain. The thing that I don't understand is when people say that they feel your pain. I can comprehend where they are going with that statement. However, if someone sticks a two-edge sword through my stomach, can another person truly say that they feel my pain? Is the sword also in their belly? Of course not! Now they may be able to sympathize or empathize with me, but not as far as feeling exactly what I'm feeling. You can only get close to the surface. That's just like the argument of whether there is a heaven.

You can't understand for anyone else, neither can you think for another person. Honestly, heaven may not be what you think it is. Most can't obtain the imagining capacity to harbor a realization of heaven. So, people guess what things should be like. After guessing for so long, they believe their assumptions.

No matter what God you serve— whether it is Buddha, Allah, Jesus Christ, Yahweh, Jehovah, or the stars and the moon, do you not think that your God is powerful enough to speak things into existence? Of course, you do! Every creation is from the creator. Think about it! Why wouldn't the self-sufficient one create a heaven? If we are made in the Lord's image we can somewhat think superior. As humans, we want our loved ones to be around us. Why wouldn't God want his children to co-exist with him in his kingdom? Surely earth is not the Lord's throne. It is his footstool. His home is where sin does not exist. In Revelation 21:2 Saint John says:

"And I saw the holy city, New Jerusalem, coming down from. God out of heaven, prepared as a bride adorned for her husband."

Then later in verses 19-22 he describes briefly what heaven looks like.

"And the foundations of the wall of the city

were garnished with all manner of precious stones.

The first foundation was Jasper, the second, sapphire;

the third, a chalcedony; the fourth, an emerald;

the fifth, sardonyx; the sixth, sardius;

the seventh, chrysolite; the eighth, Beryl;

the ninth, a topaz; the tenth, a chrysoprasus;

the eleventh, a jacinth; the twelfth, an amethyst.

And the twelve gates were twelve pearls;

every several gates were of one pearl;

and the street of the city was pure gold,

as it was transparent glass."

King Solomon is the wisest man that has ever been recorded. He said when a man dies, his body returns to the dirt and his spirit goes back to God from which it came. Now any "half-way" righteous person in their correct mind shouldn't argue with that. Now the question remains, where is God?

Ecclesiastes 5:2
"For God is in heaven, and thou upon earth;
Therefore, let thy words be few."

Now I don't know much about Muslims because I never studied Islam, yet, I do know that there are a variety of Muslims. Some believe there is a heaven and some don't. The ones that do believe call their heaven paradise. I have seen the ones that believe in strapping up with bombs. They proclaim if they execute a certain task that their God will grant them ten virgins in paradise. Now I don't know the difference between the

Muslims that believe there is a heaven from the ones that do not. I will leave that controversy to the members of that religion.

I would like to inquire if marriage or sex would even be permitted in heaven knowing that our earthly bodies would decay and be corrupt. One must understand the comparison of celestial and terrestrial bodies. A celestial body is heavenly or divine (spiritual). A terrestrial body is of the earth.

That's why to get into heaven, we must worship our savior in *spirit* and in truth (John 4:24). Folks, there will be no sex in heaven, let alone a wedding. Our natural bodies will be obliterated. When it speaks of a bride and groom being prepared like that of a marriage, that saying is symbolic, meaning the return of the promised one.

Chapter 3

Men

They are stubborn, arrogant, cocky, but strong, brilliant, and at times unchangeable. What is it so great about men that God admires? What is the purpose of creating men?

Genesis 1:26
"And God said, let us make man in our Image, after our likeness."

Genesis 1:26 is very important because it draws attention to the conclusion of many doubt and questions. The first note I would like to exploit is whom God addresses as "us" and "ours". Normally the terms "us" and "our" are used in the context in which we refer to one another or ourselves; this means one has the same motives and attributes as the being that expressed the term. I wouldn't relate to another person as "us" if I didn't have any dealing with him or her. So, who was the Lord referring to as "us" and "ours"? Was it another god as himself that He was having this assiduous conversation with? Obviously, He was conversing with someone that could create.

Now I'm not going to go any further on this subject because I would be moving too fast, as a matter of fact, the above paragraph is the primary lesson that will be discovered in the second volume of this exact book. However, what I would like to draw your attention to is how and why God created man. We were formed in His likeness. Made by the breath of His words, God is not a who but a what. The who is Jehovah, Yahweh, Allah, Jah, Buddha, Jesus Christ, Mary or whomever you call God. The "what" is His activities.

The Creator creates. Many of us create even if we are not aware of it. We create jobs, duties, problems, fun, events, responsibility, and even children. We make things happen. Believe it or not, we created the very situation that we are in today. Whether it's good or bad.

We are not puppets. Our Father has given us the power of choice. Even if options are put out in front of us, it is our decision to pick between the contrasts. The Lord wasn't fully consummated. When He created the cattle, creeping things, fowls, lights, land and water, he wanted something better. He wanted someone to rule as he did. The creator saved the best for last. He made men subjugate His creation.

Some may wonder why men are so controlling, arrogant or equipped naturally with authority. It's in us to have dominance. We are kings and nothing should be able to take away the repertoire. The only thing that has power over us is the thing that we allow to have power over us. I was once in a facility where ninety percent of the individuals were given a work assignment. What was perplexing about this is how most of the people implemented their task. Some would go out of their way to do things for their supervisors that they wouldn't dare do for themselves, not even their own mother.

Others would put their lives on the line to protect the product surrounding their job. They would start arguments if someone came near their so-called area. To me they were carrying out like hooligans over something that didn't belong to them. They didn't get paid for their labor. The products were free and not to mention plentiful. The supervisor that they went out of the way didn't have the least respect for them. They weren't even considered as humans, but they wanted so diligently to prove to their boss that they were worthy to sustain a position.

Nevertheless, in this same facility some men regulated as little as the remote controller to the television. The tube, job assignment, or anything at all did not belong to them. As a matter of fact, the exact thing that they protected could have been confiscated by the administration at anytime. They knew this and still felt the need to dictate. So, I asked myself— when people are labeled as rejects to society and everything is stripped away once they hit rock bottom, why do men still have that desire to rule? After contemplating on this question for many months it finally dawned on me; men were created to be dominate. When Elohim formed us, He put the spirit to rule in our nature. Another reason men were created was to be fruitful and multiply (Genesis 1:28).

Yes, we are supposed to have sex! How else can we multiply?

Unfortunately, some people confuse the forbidden fruit that was in the Garden of Eden. They believe that the forbidden fruit was a symbolic figure of speech. Meaning that the fruit was not an element that grew on a tree. It was a term used in the biblical days that as a form of sex. I'm here to tell you that none of that is true. How could the forbidden fruit be misconstrued as sex when God deliberately gave Adam instructions to replenish the earth?

However, sex was not meant to be carried out in the unruly way as it is today. Sex was meant to be performed as a celebration. Nowadays, people are having intercourse with another person just to get off. They have never thought of the value of virginity or saving themselves for marriage.

Yet, we wonder why we do not receive what we ask for from the Most High, or we ask why so much havoc and chaos come into our lives? We should stop and realize the things that we misuse and abuse. We take so much for granted and never pay too much attention to righteousness. In our minds, our flesh has forced us to believe that certain activities are alright. Sometimes we may even push it to the back of our brain so that we do not have to ponder on it. Our true nature is frolicked, but when we turn a positive into a negative, that's when our lives become difficult. I was taught that if you always do what you've always done then you'll always get what you've always gotten.

Another reason our lives become complicated is because we try to do too much at one time. When several things are thrown at us we try to tackle them all at once instead of handling them individually.

Learn to minimize the situations so it could be viewed for what it really is.

Blowing things out of proportion will have you hallucinating. Now I am not saying this for you to be lazy or idle minded. I am subsequently saying that we are supposed to rest.

God is the perfect example; read Genesis 2:3.

The glorious one knows that when we don't rest from our work, our bodies will shut down. We are not machines. We become tiresome. Continuing to work will make our judgment cloudy. I understand that some people are workaholics. Their addiction to work keeps their mind from being flustered on other things.   Society teaches people to work all day then play at night.

They proclaim that there isn't any time to rest, so some say they will sleep when they die. The concept of revenue, expenses, and assets controls their drive to stay active. Contrary to your belief, imagine the blessings that we will receive if we loan a lot of that grinding time to worshipping, praising, or meditating on the creator's word.

Chapter 4

Women

Can't live with them and can't live without them. You must love them even though you don't want to be around them sometimes. Women are God's precious gift to men. Have we disvalued, disrespected, and neglected this jewel?

Our savior is so great that he allowed men to inherit the earth. Genesis 19:1 says that the Lord brought all creatures to Adam and let him name them. How selfless is that? Since the beginning of time the supreme one was a giving Lord. Not only is he considerable, he knows exactly what to grant us. He gave us the greatest gift on earth a help meet. However, there's a saying in this world that quotes, "Men can't live with women and women can't live without men." Well, maybe the ones that can't live with them don't understand the true nature of a woman. Ladies are a precious and beautiful motivation to men. She is our helper and mate. She helps us acquire our goals and capture our dreams. She is meant to meet us halfway with our requirements. Although she is the weaker vessel, her reflection should be a reflection of our strength. Nowadays, people are insisting that women keep the world populated. Women do give birth to boys and girls, but individuals forgot that women were created by men, for men, and of men (Gen. 2:21-23). If it were not for the rib of Adam then woman would not exist in the first place.

There are two things that I know for sure about a woman. One is that she was created because man was lonely (Gen. 2:18). The other is that females are subject to the sound of a man's voice. There is a king in every man that causes the woman to tremble at the sound of His voice. Women are compassionate, sweet, thoughtful, and idealists. Some are in depth to fear although they may have a bad or snobbish attitude at times.

At the end of the day they are still women. In the book of Genesis, the serpent knew that Eve had a soft spot. He knew that that Eve would take the bait if he presented his manipulation adequately. Do you have to ask yourself the prominent question? Why would Satan test Eve instead of Adam? That's simple. He was aware of who the weaker vessel was. He knew at the right time with the right line that she would be easy going or perhaps naive and gullible. Though Eve was not necessarily his primary target, he knew that to get to someone you have to go through the person that is closest to them first. He also knew that it's not all about the message that you are presenting, but the presentation of the message. Satan twisted his words when speaking to the woman, and she fell for the "old banana in the tail pipe". Not only did she fall for it, she took the man out right along with her. Still until this day the way to get to most men is to go through his woman. Think about it. Majority of the crimes that happen is because a woman was somewhere involved. I'm not saying that she was present at the scene. Either a guy did the crime trying to impress a woman or he was trying to remove an obstacle out of the way that blocked him from getting next to her.

God stoically knew the weight that women acquired, so he multiplied her sorrow by inscribing pain whenever she gave birth (Gen 3:16). Not only was child labor compensation for her violation, but her next punishment was what most people do not like to talk about. Her next punishment was what I would like for us to dwell on.

Genesis 3:16
*"... and thy desire
shall be to thy husband,
and he shall rule over thee."*

This verse is twofold. I always wondered why a man would speak so foul to a woman, treat her bad, or beat her with his fist and she return back to that same relationship. She may hope that the situation would change but deep down in the back of her mind she knew that it wouldn't. Well, the reason why she felt trapped by this man was because she desired this man. She desired him so badly that her securities and everything else was placed on the back burner.

Women are attention seekers. Some feel that if you don't show them enough attention, then you don't love them and they will do things that aggravate you. If it's obnoxious, their real intent is just to gain your focus, but some men take it the wrong way and blow it out of proportion because they don't understand the motive behind a woman's action.

A lot of women seek after a man because they didn't have a father present in their lives when they were growing up.

They feel that they need a male figure to be in their life and so they may go after that companionship the wrong way. They submit to having sex with a man repeatedly because of the absence of a father that can never be fulfilled in its entirety. Some women seek that affection that they feel they are lacking. Some women even grow up to hate all men because of what their dad, stepdad, or a close relative did to them.

Another thing that I have always speculated on is why women engage in intimacy with another man after a relationship. I know some women that will break with their boyfriend and then by the end of two weeks she has already committed to another boyfriend. There are a percentage of people who are nympho's. A spirit has taken a toll on them and caused them to have sex repeatedly with several different men. Most of them feel like they can't live without having a man in their life. They just need someone to cling their heart onto. Perhaps, they feel a void if the presence of a male isn't around them. They mourn for their compliments and attention. No matter how you look at it, the facts are inevitable. So, the next time that your family member, associate, or friend returns to an abusive relationship, know that it isn't futile. It's simply the curse that has been since the start of time.

Furthermore, another part of the woman's desire for a man is half of the reason why homosexuals exist. Confusion is set up in their mind and it conveys into imitating male attributes. They try to act, walk, and talk like a man. However, not all women that have this desire are lesbians. Some are as womanly as they could be. They are just possessive and want to rule like a man. They are controlling, aggressive, and believe that men are a product or some type of boy toy that was created specifically for them. They prefer to be the head of the relationship and downgrade the men as the submissive one. This is really a mockery to creation.

Some women have gotten so iron scalded and bold that a man can't tell them anything. It's shameful how some portray parenting as being both the mother and the father. Women alone are taking on the role as the father is understandably harsh. They must have a split personality to accomplish both roles. This encounter does not always have the children dysfunctional, but maybe rather confused.

However, it is not supposed to be like this. Over thousands and thousands of years the world has become tangled and twisted. It is no longer coherent to reality. The true intentions of things have been reversed or thrown off track.

Chapter 5

Relationships

Relationships are not what they used to be. It's not about love or finding your soul mate anymore. It's about going half on the bills. They are not based on the brains, spirituality, and inner beauty. It's about who has the nicest things and who has the biggest booty. Who is the cutest, most paid, or packing? I couldn't go any longer in this book without getting on the case of relationships. So, you call yourself in a relationship huh?!? What is your role in the relationship? What position are you in? Whose authority are you under? Some say that they are men because of the physical strength that they possess or because they have a penis attached to their body. Let me tell you something, a horse has testicles and a bull has the strength of an ox, does that make them a man? Of course not! Our first role as a man is to be responsible, independent, and have our priorities in order.

> Genesis 2:15
> "And the Lord God took the man,
> and put him into the garden of Eden
> to dress it and to keep it."

Since the beginning of time, if a man didn't work he couldn't eat. God acknowledges our manhood. He knows that we would grow idle minded if our days didn't consist of responsibilities. Our first job was to cultivate the Garden of Eden. What's so ironic about tending to our priorities is that God's immediate stimulus was for Adam to till the ground from whence he was taken (Gen. 3:23). Our role as men is to be a provider for our wife and children. Not only are we to put food on the table, we are to make sure that they stay aligned with God's plan. We are to set the examples in the way they ought to live. For we are the head of our wives (Ephesians 5:23). Subsequently, our wife is the head of our children. When we see her, we ought to see a reflection of the God within us. Therefore, her teaching and nurturing of the children will be like a chain reaction. However, although the scriptures indicate men as the head, some people misconstrue the actual meaning.

Some men automatically think that being the head means that the opposite sex is supposed to be subjugated, humiliated, or ordered at the demand of his masculinity. That is not so. This description of humane is what you call a paradox— a contradicting abstract statement that is nevertheless the truth. That's why men beat, manipulate, and verbally abuse their women. They already feel that they are supposed to be head of the relationship. Their desire to dominate is confused with control issues.

Misplaced dominance is what I call it.

Putting your hands on another person only makes the situation worse. If a lady was a certain way before you met her then you have chosen to be with her and you should deal with whatever it is in a civil manner. If she has changed on you, perhaps you should figure out why she has changed, and then figure out if you should stay or move on.

Beating on women and verbally abusing them is a bad example for your children and others around you. **Imagine how God feels when you are mistreating the gift that He has given to you.**

If the shoe were on the other foot, how would you feel? Sympathize with her emotions. How would you feel if you were the woman and she was the man acting out the way you do? Think about how it intimidates the children. Some things get old and at times people get fed up.

What happens when she leaves for good? What if you accidentally kill her? What if she kills you?!

I saw a relationship where a man abused his woman several times. I will not allow myself to say that the drugs and alcohol was an excuse for this guy's actions.

However, I will say that chemical imbalances do play a major part in one's ability to function properly. At the same time, the person knew what kind of effect that those drugs and alcohol would have before they partook in them. This guy acted out so belligerently that it got to the point where his children were afraid of him. Not only that, but his girlfriend was a good woman. It was not until he perpetually accused her of cheating when she ran off with another man. The sad part of this story is that when she left him, everything began to go downhill for him. He couldn't pay his bills, he started robbing people and his drug addictions increased. Worst of all, he finally realized that he loved and missed her and the children so much that he literally started going insane.

All of this happened because he wanted to control another person with misplaced dominance. Men and women, you cannot dictate people or change them. Let God change them. You can only plant the seed and maybe someone else will have to keep it watered. Only God gives the increase for that seed to blossom into a beautiful human being.

When the creator formed men in His image, He gave us dominion over every living and non-living thing.

There is no one greater than the molder Himself. Unfortunately, all of that was thrown away because of sin. Our disobedience has always put us in a situation that is fatal and detrimental to our health. For example, how weak was Adam to fall for Eve's ignorance? Instead of him being a man and stepping up to the plate, he compromised. What he should have said was "Eve, I'm putting my foot down."

God only gave us one rule to abide by and that was to not eat from the forbidden tree. So, I'm not going to eat that fruit and neither are you.

God has been good to us for us to go against His word. After He created the heavens and the earth, He saved the best thing for last. He created male and female. There was one work ethic required of us before the beginning of time and before humans were formed.

Genesis 2:5
"For the Lord God has not caused
it to rain upon the earth,
and there was not a man to till the ground."

God already knew that work would be required of man. The book of Genesis later explains that God planted a garden eastward in Eden and there He put the man whom He had formed. Jehovah knew every inch of the earth. He understood every mount and every valley. Yet, He didn't place the man anywhere else except where He planted the garden. Just like people today like their gardens to look good, so did God. That's why He took man and put Him into the Garden of Eden *to dress it and to keep it.*

Genesis 2:20
"But for Adam there was not
found a helper comparable to him."

True enough, God created woman because

man was lonely (Gen. 2:18). The good Lord felt sympathy for us. He wanted someone to assist us in achieving our needs. God did not make women for men to abuse and mistreat them. If you don't believe me, then read your bible.

Womanizing is not in fashion.

No matter how much rappers rap about the degrading of another human being or singers sing about this disgrace. It is just not right— even if you grew up with parents that would argue and fight all the time.

Some women start to believe that fighting and sexing shortly after is a way of life. You shouldn't accept the abuse because that is what your mom, sister, aunt, grandma, or any other person close to you went through. Men, dad was wrong and had very low self-esteem if he was the type to abuse a woman. **Only insecurities bring about violence. Maybe you ought to check yourself to see where the faultiness lies.**

The reason why most of us have problems in our relationship is because our spouse isn't compatible with us. They may lack intelligence, communication, faithfulness, personality, ethics, morals, sensitivity, financial support, etc.

However, as humans we take the worldly approach in searching for a soul mate. Men may want a woman with a pretty face, voluptuous body, or cute feet. Ladies may enjoy their significant other to have money, fine cars, a big shoe size, or one that is tall and dark. Whatever the preference is, we must realize that it is merely lust. When we confuse love for lust then many obstacles occur.

One thing that we must understand is that love is broken down into six types. These six types of love are sexual, brotherly, unconditional, sacrificial, and surprising love. They are all diverse types of love that I will explain to you in the next few pages of this book. If you are in a relationship right now, as you read the different meanings, try to identify which type of love you are in and which type you want to be in.

Sexual love – Lust. This kind of love is at the sake of pleasure. This kind of love permits couples who can't get along to stay together. They cannot stand to see each other with another person and they are sex whipped. If you have ever been sprung, or had someone whipped before, then you know what sexual love is.

Brotherly love – Everyone that you like is not meant to be your spouse or mate. Some people are just meant to be your friend. You can love them as a brother or sister.

Unconditional love – Also called agape love. This is when you love a person regardless of their condition. You forgive their wrong doings and look over their flaws and mishaps. You are willing to work situations out and make a natural bond forever lasting. This is the type of love that is talked about in marriage vows. For better or for worse is the key. Through thick and thin, surviving the good and the bad. It is the type of love that God has. Do you have it?

Sacrificial love – Putting loved ones before you. Jesus Christ is the perfect example of sacrifice love. Most people are not willing to accept a loss so they don't have sacrificial love. You must lose to win again. Are you willing to accept a loss?

Selfish love – It's all about you. You don't focus on your spouse's point of views. You only see things your way. You seem to think that the world revolves around you. You should always be open to other's feelings and point of views. Are you?

Surprising love – This is a confused relationship. This happens when you are dealing with someone who's mood swings a lot. You perpetually go through ups and downs and ins and outs or deal with someone who does odd things and keeps you off your toes. All surprising love isn't negative. A lot of it is good, fun, and nurturing.

However, when you don't know what to expect out of a person, that is surprising love!

Notice in Gen. 1:27, God created male and female. However, the Provider didn't make just any type of female for Adam. Adam was something like God's main man, his homeboy, or his protégé. The Lord formed a wife specifically for him. (Gen 1:18-25).

Sadly, the people of today's time go running after the first woman or man that they see look halfway decent. It wasn't meant to be like this. Adam had to be patient, worthy, delicate, and pure until his soul mate conjured.

The same way as Elohim brought Eve to Adam (Gen 2:22). We ought to trust the creator to bring a person into our life that is ripe and suitable for us. Somewhere, somehow, that unique individual is out there and they are made specifically for us. However, if we jump at the first thing that looks presentable then we might miss our inherent blessing.

Everything that glitters isn't gold.

The grass isn't always greener on the other side. It may look decent far off. Yet, after a lot of time and energy has been invested we discover that either we rushed and got our own way or we allowed someone else to block the passage that was meant for us to take. Don't be eager to settle. Take your time. Be patient and remember that it's never too late to improve. **You can always be diligent, but at the same time, make the correct choices.** Believe me, it's not all about pleasure. Fun can get you into a world of trouble. Anything worth having is worth waiting for, and anything worth having is worth working for or working with.

God wants us to have joy.

The thing about joy is that it is something that is embedded into you. No one can take the joy you have away from you regardless of what is going on. You see, people misconstrue joy with happiness, not knowing that being happy and having joy is two different components. To be happy, you must have something happening. Perhaps, the movies, dinner, a gift, or some sort of service will make you happy. However, when those elements fade away, you are not happy anymore. That's why it is best to have joy. In the midst of a storm, the joy your significant other provides will bring you through. Now I'm not saying all of this for you to give up on your current partner.

I Corinthians 7:13-14
"And the woman which hath an husband
that believeth not, and if he be pleased to dwell
with her, let her not leave him.
For the unbelieving husband is sanctified
by the wife, and the unbelieving
wife is sanctified by the husband;
else were your children unclean;
but now they are holy."

At times, we can entice someone to be who we want them to be, or even who the Awesome One wants them to be. Giving up too easy sets one up for low self-esteem. Look out for others, but at the same time respect your own mind frame. If you aren't stable, surely you can't be beneficial to anyone else's well being. What I'm saying is, don't make foolish decisions.

Whether your selection is self-proclaimed, sacrificial, manipulative, coerced, rushed, or just something that you want to do at that time. The universal law is cause and effect. Your actions that are made from here on out will have a major impact on your future.

I Corinthians 11:8-9
"For the man is not of the woman;
but the woman of the man.

THE Inner VOICE

Neither was the man created for the woman; but the woman for the man."

Verse 11 says:
"Nevertheless, neither is the man
without the woman;
neither the woman without
the man, in the Lord."

God loves unity for it is strength in numbers. Like the Apostle Paul says, "I say therefore to the unmarried and widows, it is good for them if they abide even as I" (I Corinthians 7:8). This means that God can do so much more with you if you are single!

Chapter 6

Souls and Spirits

Are souls and spirits a fantasy? What about Ghosts? If souls and spirits are a reality then what is the difference between the two?

The mind is the most powerful element that ever existed on this earth. It can make you into who you were designed to be or it can break you down alienate you. Your thought process challenges the mind to be very beneficial or critical. Like I mentioned before, we are not puppets! We can choose options. Everything that was ever formed was built from some form of thought process. Think about it! It has been recorded that God said, "Let there be light," and then there was light. Then God separated the darkness from the light. Even the fowls, grass, and humans that were originally created were first a thought process.

God processed His thoughts, spoke it, and then gave life to it.

On a lower scale, everything man made was first perceived in the mind. A house or building isn't formatted without a blueprint, and a blueprint is merely thoughts that are written and drawn out. Why do you think that banks want to business plans, diagrams, blueprints, or portfolios before they consider granting you a loan? That's simple. They desire to see your full vision in its entirety. Just speaking out about your thoughts are totally different than seeing them.

> Habakkuk 2:2-3
> "And the Lord answered me, and said,
> write the vision, make it plain upon tables,
> that he may run that readeth it.
> For the vision is yet for an appointed time,
> but at the end it shall speak, and not lie;
> though it tarry, wait for it;
> *because it will surely come, it will not tarry,*"

Have you ever heard of the saying, "speak things into existence"? Well, writing your visions out thoroughly on paper is another form of speaking your mind into the realization of it. Time after time, I have heard people say that they see this or that in the spiritual realm but it has not manifested into the natural yet. I used to ask God why it has not been made to manifest yet. It's been declared in heaven, but I don't see any results of it on earth yet.

True enough, Jehovah is on His own timing and surely His ways and thoughts supersedes ours. Yet, the Most High wants our heart and mind to be ready for what he has in store for us.

The mind can be very tricky. If you don't watch it you can out-wit yourself. I have seen people whose brains were too large for the small towns that they lived in. Therefore, nothing got accomplished. I have seen some of the smartest people turn to drugs and alcohol because they allowed their minds to be succumb to what they figured would take them to a higher level, not knowing that a natural high was an obscured route. My people, consider yourself wise and tap into the full capacity of your brain. Some have never nor will they ever reach the full percentage if their thinking ability. The flesh has blinded them from seeing further than they are supposed to see. The enemy has deceived them into believing that they are no more than what they appear to be. Frivolous gods have muffled their ears from hearing the truth.

In the famous words of Dr. Martin Luther King, the mind is a terrible thing to waste. It can be very superficial or dramatic. Imagine, if you could change the way you think, then your behavior will change. When your behavior has changed then your actions will start to transform. Once your actions have evolved then your lifestyle will begin to alternate. As your lifestyle is being reformed, the people that are around your lifestyle will gradually began to mutate. However, the process all began with the thinking in your own mind. So, the next time you are wondering why the people around you have not adjusted, you need to step up and lead by example. Honestly, it may be a while before they fully adapt, but be patient. You can only reap harvests in due season.

Ephesians 4:23
"And be renewed In the spirit, of
your mind."

I was in meditation one day and heard a voice say to walk in the spirit is the fixation of your mind. This was ironic because some people tend to think that when it says we ought to walk in the spirit, that means that an alien takes over our mind, body, and soul; when fingers are snapped, we are supposed to do everything according to a hypnosis. Yes, the holy spirit does take over our presence. The feeling is unexplainable. However, it is far more than an intoxication that any earthly substance can give off. My advice to people that are popping pills, snorting cocaine, smoking crack or weed, shooting up with heroin, or drinking alcohol is to try God's highest heights. A mere high is nothing compared to feeling ethereal!

To walk in the spirit of our mind can either limit, stagger, or broaden our boundaries.

The fixation is our ability to be molded adequately. For the clay does not say to the potter, "Fix me this way," but the potter says to the clay "I will see to you this way." Whether you believe it or not, our mind is powerful enough to heal our own body of sickness. Yet, on that same token, if we tell our body that it is about to die, nine times out of ten the hallucination will take over and decompose your body. I know we have heard the phrase "As a man thinketh so is he." (Proverbs 23:7) That saying is true in so many instances.

We can speak life or death into situations, people, or events. Uprisings and downfalls are in the authority of the tongue. Remember that God made us into His image, and just like He formed the world, we have those same capabilities to create our reality.

We are gods! Did you fret because I said we are gods? We are. I am a god and you are also a god. However, don't misconstrue what I recently said. We are not the big God because there is only one God. We are the lowercase g-o-d.

John 10:30-35
"I and my father are one. Then the Jews took up stones again to stone him.
Jesus answered them,
"Many good works have I shown you from my father, for which of those works do ye stone me? The Jews answered him;
saying, for a good work we stone thee not; but for blasphemy; and because that thou, being a man, makest thyself God.
Jesus answered them, is it not written in your law, I said, ye are gods? If he called them gods, unto whom the word of God came, and the scripture cannot be broken."

Likewise, have you ever thought about being sick then the illness suddenly comes upon you? Have you thought about being fired or suspended from a job, and then it happened? When was the last time you were thinking of something good or terrible happening? Know that the very thing that you imagine or speak will be upon you because you fathomed the elements through your thoughts or breath. It is not a coincidence. Images appear from imaginations. Words speak life into revelation.

Now that I have introduced you to minds in this chapter, allow me to take further down the avenue in which I really intended to travel, which are souls and spirits! For us to fully understand souls and spirits, we must first break it down for what they really are. Souls and spirits are not some big magical globe like substance that some people pretend it to be. A soul is merely your appetite, desires, deep feelings, or emotions that you have.

That's why your soul can become vexed after dealing with troubling people or troubling situations for so long. Do you get what I'm saying? Your soul consists of the things that you mourn for! Although, it is also conceived as the immortal part of a person. Have you ever been aloof from a person but felt the same thing that they felt? Maybe someone close to you could have passed away, but at certain times, it seems as if a portal field draws you to coincide with them? The soul is immortal because it never dies. A mother is well connected with her soul and the soul of her children. You don't have to tell your mother what's wrong sometimes. She can sense it before it happens or before you tell her. I'm not say that this the case in every circumstance, but at times, it is.

Most people say that the eyes are the window to the soul. People can fix their mouths to say anything or make facial expressions. Believe what you want to. However, the eyes reveal the deepest, darkest secrets. The eyes make known the true intentions of the soul.

Ecclesiastes 12:7
"Then shall the dust return to the earth
 as it was; and the spirit return unto God who
 gave it."

Earlier I mentioned about the spirit of your mind. Majority of the times when it talks about your spirit or heart in the Bible, it is referring to the fixation of your mind. Whether it is good or bad, evil or not, it is mainly up to you. The spirit is somewhat like the soul, but it differs in certain aspects. It's what I like to call *tangent*—meaning it's touching on the same subject but drawn away by details. Spirit is mind and mind is spirit. Imagine when a neurologist cracks open a skull to examine or operate on one's brain. Once the cranium is parted, he can see the components that makes up the brain.

However, there is one thing that he can't see, and that is the mind. Truthfully, no carnality can visualize your mind. People may assume things about you without you expressing it to them. Yet, the only one that can see the things that no one else can see *is* the only One that no one can see.

What fleshly person can scrutinize your conscious, intellect, opinions, creativity, or reasoning?

They may be able to take an educated guess and luckily their hypothesis ends up being accurate. However, in no way, shape, form, or fashion can anyone on God's green earth view your mind. It has never been recorded in history and it will never be recorded. The spirit governs your attributes and endeavors. Whether you know it or not, behind every motive is a higher dominion. It just transforms actions through a humanly form.

It's like when you convince, motivate, coerce, or manipulate someone else into doing a particular thing.

A spirit is very powerful.

It's been recorded that some people blackout and don't know what they had done when the spirit conveyed. By the time that they come back, the mishap has already happened. All spiritual takeovers are not bad; during the transaction, some people get healed, speak in tongues, prophesy, and teach things that wouldn't be possible with their own will.

The battle between good and evil is a devastating warfare.

There is no other war like the one going on in the mass majorities mind. Some will win their preferred side, and others will compromise. To the people that don't believe that there is a heaven or God, do you believe that when life is taken out of your body that your spirit dies? Think outside the box because some things are forever lasting!

Chapter 7

Fasting

What's the purpose of starving yourself? Do you lose weight when fasting?

Joel 2:12
"Therefore, also now, saith the Lord,
turn ye even to me with all your heart,
and with fasting, and with weeping,
and with mourning."

We should know that our spirit is what intercedes with the "Great I Am That I Am". At no time can your flesh communicate to *Abba*. Our flesh is contaminated and unworthy to connect with something so precious and valuable as the spirit. Fasting kills the flesh so we can be in tune with our inner being. Without fasting, we are incapable of clearly hearing the Master when He speaks. God wants our attention.

Even though many attractions hinder us from fully paying attention. Whether we know it or not. There are only three different voices that squall around in our head. They may sound different at times, but in reality, the inner voices are only characterized into three different socials— one of course, is our Heavenly Father.

The other is the enemy or as we like to call him, the devil. The last attribute in our head is our own voice better known as the flesh. The best way to distinguish the most significant vocal is by sacrificing. Fasting blocks out the unnecessary things so that we can be the sheep that knows our Lord's voice. Once we can decipher the Most High's voice from the other voices, we can grow into our purpose more genuinely. Knowing our purpose means more divine blessings.

Even in the natural realm, we know that communication is key. How much more eminent is conversing in the spiritual realm? Very much important. Of course, we want to know our reason for being here on earth, and the best way to find the meaning of our life is to ask the one that started life. Our purpose for being born wasn't only to live, pay bills, and die. Surely, it's not merely meant to struggle, sell dope, prostitute, tell lies, gang-bang, live to stay on top of every other human being, or live paycheck to paycheck. Of course, we are supposed to take care of our responsibilities, work to eat, and chase after our goals or dreams.

However, somewhere amongst handling our responsibilities there is a void that needs to be filled on the inside. If you search deep down inside, you will discover this void I'm mentioning; this void is the exact reason why some people become bored. The reason for this is because they haven't stepped into their calling. Their dynamic purpose has not surfaced yet. Now you may ask why! It's because you haven't done what was required to get your assignment from God.

Fasting and praying goes hand and hand. It is the best way to get answers and speed up miracles. Back in the ancient days, great prophets would fast and extravagant things would happen. In the Book of Esther, she was willing to die (Esther 4:15-16). She commanded her people to fast along with her before she boldly went amongst the king with her requirements. If you know the story of Esther then you know that fasting brought forth favor.

Moses fasted in the mountains for 40 days and 40 nights before the ten commandments were hand written by God (Exodus 34:28). Daniel fasted for three entire weeks before a vision came to him and it was made known that his words were honored by God (Daniel 10:2-12). When the disciples of Christ couldn't cast out a demonic force in a young boy, the father of the child brought him to Jesus. Jesus instantly commanded the deaf and dumb spirit to come out of the boy and never return again. Once the spirits had fled, the disciples inquired unto Jesus asking why they couldn't rebuke the seizures, foaming at the boy's mouth, and gnashing of teeth. Christ said, "This kind can come forth by nothing, but by prayer and fasting." (Mark 9: 29)

Now, no one ever said fasting would be easy. As a matter of fact, hardly anything easy has a valuable impact. During the period of fasting, you are going to be hungry or thirsty. Some people are even drowsy and tired.

The test is to endure the hardship.

As time goes on, you become more familiar and equipped to handle the disadvantages. I remember when I used to smoke cigarettes. I used to think the hardest thing to do was to stop smoking cigarettes. I tried many times to go cold turkey but I failed. I quit for days one time and thought that I had it beat, but before I knew it I was right back holding onto a filter with my lips; what made the situation worse is that I smoked more than I did before I stopped. It was like I was trying to make up for the days that I didn't smoke.

Eventually, I had sit and thought to myself for a moment or two. I said, "I have tried to stop smoking about ten times now. So why can't I stop?" After contemplating on the matter, I finally came to a conclusion. The reason why I stopped then started back so many times before was because I didn't have my mind made up to truly quit. I had wanted to quit for all the wrong reasons, and I was lying to myself. Deep down in my heart I really didn't want to, I was just saying I wanted to. Moreover, I finally stopped smoking five years ago. I don't even have the craving anymore. People smoke around me all the time and it doesn't affect me because I have my mind made up to never ever take a drug from those poison vapors again. I didn't mean to take your mind from the subject of fasting.

I told you about the story of the cigarettes because it sort of ties in with my encouragement of fasting. You see, putting a stop to smoking cigarettes was one of the hardest things to do. I was addicted to those nasty chemicals for almost

17 years. I thought that I would never quit, but by the grace of God anything can be accomplished.

To fast properly, you have to have your mind made up to do so. Nothing must persuade you or hinder you from doing what is required. Hunger pains are going to attack you. Your body will attempt to manipulate you to stop fasting. That's why the Word says that the spirit is willing but the flesh is weak. When you fast, your flesh wars against your spirit and your spirit battles against your flesh. Which one you will win is entirely up to you. Just know that only one can win.

The thing about overcoming the addiction to cigarettes is knowing that the cravings will come. That's irrefutable, but in order to overcome the cravings you have to be prepared and know that they will only last for about 5 minutes at a time.

If you can get past those five minutes the cravings come, then victory will be yours! The same concept applies when it comes to fasting. Cravings are going to come. They may even come perpetually. Yet, if you master the art of withstanding, then you have won a very important match.

As time goes by, your fighting ability becomes more strategic. Everyone's technique isn't the same, but your skills will enhance—developing a more proficient and efficient way to conquer the challenge. When you are fasting, the enemy comes upon you suddenly when you least expect it. Demons come at you harder to discourage you from completing your goals. You must have a made-up mind that nothing and no one will detour you from your achievement.

The first time that I chose to fast for 50 days straight, people came off to me in a way that they never have before. The first day was awkward because I had to bite my tongue. The following day, an officer and another guy tried to create an argument with me. Usually, I would have indulged into their malarkey. Yet, I stayed humble and let the tempting flame pass over. The word tells us that we will be tried by fire, but before gold is crafted it must be melted by heat (I Peter 1:7). What I am saying is that for us to evolve, it takes humility. Being the bigger person does not always make you feel good. When you are fasting, people are going to disrespect you. They are going to lash out at you. They are going to crawl under your skin. Just know that long suffering is a fruit of the Spirit. Also know that it's not actually the person that is attacking you. Sometimes the person does not realize what they are doing to you.

Even Jesus Christ said "...forgive them, for they know not what they do." (Luke 23:34) Nevertheless, we must endure until the end.

Matthew 6:16-18

"Moreover, when ye fast, be not, as the hypocrites, of a sad countenance; for they disfigure their faces, that they may appear unto men to fast. Verily I say unto you, they have their reward. But thou, when thou fasteth, anoint thine head, and wash thy face. That thou appear not unto men to fast, but unto thy father which is in secret; and thy father, which seeth in secret, shall reward thee openly."

Fasting is not meant to be displayed like we are doing some great service to God. The Lord of Host could have the rocks and dirt to praise him if he wanted to.

It's a trip how people fast and broadcast it like they want the entire world to know. Now, I don't think there's anything wrong if you tell certain people about your fast. However, it is wrong when you try to get the glory for fasting.

You want people to "toot your horn" because you are going days without eating or drinking. **A fast is between you and the Glorious One.**

It's really no one else's business unless you have to mention it to avoid chaos or complaints. For instance, let's say I work as a chef; cooks are supposed to taste their own food to know what ingredients need to be added. Yet, I am on a 50 day fast. I will tell my coworkers to taste the food for me. If they are curious enough to ask why I don't want to taste my own cooking, I will explain to them that I am fasting.

I don't tell my co-workers that I'm fasting to boast and brag. I tell them for the simple fact to be honest and keep confusion down. Your revelation may be different than mine, but whatever the matter is, I believe if you are sincere, God will understand why you revealed what you and Him have going on.

I must reveal to you that abstaining from food and drinks is not the only way to fast. Fasting is about whatever is blocking your divine connection from God. If you spend most of your days watching television, you must cut the tube off for a day or so to focus more on what is pure. A lot of people play board games, dominoes, or cards. Therefore, you must eradicate that time to meditate on God's word. Now, this next one is a hard one for today's world, but it must be done. We must put down those electronics as part of our fasting. Cell phones, iPods, iPads, tablets, X-box's, and Nintendo's are a total distraction from hearing the words of God.

Facebook, Instagram, and Twitter should be eliminated from the equation also. I know a lot of you are probably second guessing this now, but if you want blessings, miracles, and changes to happen then you must sacrifice. With every pain or hardship leaving your possession is a strength and success that will be gained. Like the saying says, *no pain no gain.*

I do not want to be at a standstill all my life. I like to move forward. Yes, the ride may be bumpy and long, but the journey is much needed. If you haven't fasted yet, maybe you are scared, but you must start somewhere. I asked my youngest sister Tichina if she wanted to say anything to the readers in my book. She thought about it for a while then she said yes. She said to tell everyone that they don't have to go full force at the beginning of their fast. She explained that people can start off by trying three hours at a time for starters.

Once you have that three hours down pack then you move the hours up until you get an entire day in. Which is ironic for two reasons. One is because the same theory that she exclaimed is the same one I mentioned earlier about not being stagnant. The other reason why this is ironic is because my little sister is the one that inspired and aspired me too fast.

One day my little sister and my mother came to visit me. They both were on a 21 day fast. I was in awe because I was looking at my sibling and said to myself, "She don't weigh a hundred pounds soaking wet. There isn't any way I'm going to let a girl beat me out and she's younger than me." I can look back at that story and laugh now because it really is funny the way I said it. The moral of the story is that my motivation came when I least expected. I figured in my heart that if little sis could do it, then so could I.

Truthfully, I was afraid and nervous about fasting at first. I didn't think that I could go any length of time without eating— let alone drinking. Once I put my mind to it, I believed, then I achieved. Now I know it isn't anything to it but to do it!

Isaiah 58:3-6
"Wherefore have we fasted,
say they, and thou seest not?
Wherefore have afflicted our soul,
and thou takest no knowledge?

Behold, in the day of your fast
ye find pleasure and exact all your labours.
Behold, ye fast for strife and debate,
and to smite with the fist of wickedness;
ye shall not fast as ye do this day,
to make your voice to be heard on high.
Is it such a fast that I have chosen?
A day for a man to afflict his soul?
Is it to bow down his head as a bulrush,
and to spread sack cloth and ashes under him?
Wilt thou call this a fast,
and an acceptable day to the Lord?
Is not this the fast that I have chosen?
To loose the bands of wickedness,
to undo the heavy burdens,
and to let the oppressed go free,
and that ye break every yolk?"

The benefits of fasting are very crucial. Some
of us have spiritual wickedness in high places
warring against us that we are unaware of. Fasting
equips us with the whole amour of God. It is my
belief that when we fast it is a weapon of choice.
Naturally fighting a spirit is futile. We have to
visit that realm in order to prepare for battle. Just
like the word of *El-Shaddai* represents a sword in
the spiritual realm and our faith is symbolic for a

shield. Fasting is a stronghold, like a house where our strength is prepped for combat. Fasting is the training of the mind, body, and soul.

We must first learn how to *war* before we war. Warfare is real. It is not a game. It is not a joke. There is so much more going on in the invisible world than we can imagine. That is why Ephesians 6:12 says, "For we wrestle not against flesh and blood, but against principalities, against powers, against the rulers of darkness of this world, against spiritual wickedness in high places." We are on the battlefield for our children, parents, spouses, friends, and other relatives. We stand in the gap on their behalf by fasting. Sometimes, our loved ones don't realize what they are up against.

After reading this book you should know. At times, fasting defeats illness, death, cancer, HIV, heart attacks, strokes, and other health issues. It restores us back to our original state and other things that have we been dismantled from. Yet, the key is being sincere, whole-hearted, faithful, sinless, and consistent. However, a full recovery is not always the case in certain situations.

In II Samuel 12:15-22, David fasted for a lengthy amount of time. He fasted in high hopes that God would spare a little child's life. David did all that he was supposed to do, but the child still died. True enough, David was sad along with many other people. Unfortunately, we must know that everything we plan and hope for is not always meant to be. God has other plans even though we may feel that our way and thoughts are right. We don't get what we fast for at times because some are like the Pharisee who thought too highly of himself.

Luke 18:10-14
"Two men went into the temple to pray;
the one a Pharisee, and the other a publican.
The Pharisee stood and prayed thus with
himself, God, I thank thee, that I am not as
other men are, extortioners, unjust, adulterers,
or even as this publican.
I fast twice in the week, I give tithes of all that
I possess.
And the publican, standing afar off,
would not lift up so much as his eyes unto
heaven, but smote upon his breast, saying,
God be merciful to me a sinner.
I tell you, this man went down to his house
justified rather than the other;
For everyone that exalteth himself shall be
abased; and he that humbleth himself shall be
exalted."

We cannot compare our spiritual blessings with anyone else.

What God has for us is for us. What he has provided for another person is for them. A selfish and ungrateful person shouldn't think that they deserve anything major. Part of fasting is the ability to work on ourselves. It's to reveal the weakness's and flaws in ourselves so that so that we can rectify them. A woman once told me that if you are fasting but not spending more time with God, then you are fasting in vain.

How true her statement was.

All I am saying is that we should step up our game and stop "half-stepping".

If we are going to do anything then we must go all the way with it. Sometimes we should be willing to give up something for us to gain something else. With the ultimate sacrifice comes the ultimate miracle. If you are expecting a miracle, you must realize that miracles are birthed around great obstacles. For us to tread upon these obstacles and overcome these hurdles is through fasting. Faith alone may not break a generational curse. That's why the word tells us that faith without works is dead (James 2:20). Our works consists of obedience and fasting.

I know that this next statement that I am about

to make is about to bust some of your bubbles or make you get into your feelings a bit. However, praying is not enough sometimes. Don't get me wrong, it is always good to pray. A lot of prayers have been answered. Yet, what I am saying is for certain occasions or for some people. Praying alone will not get what you need. Therefore, Jesus Christ says in Matthew 21:17, "How beit this kind goeth not out but by prayer and fasting?" The disciples couldn't rebuke the evil spirits only by praying, so what makes you think that you can?

These are the same spirits today that were here over two thousand years ago. They may now be wiser and stronger. So, we must add fasting to our faith and prayers. Some people have prayed for many years, days, and hours, but still have not received what they have asked for. This is because they do not fast and wonder why they have not gotten any breakthroughs.

If your child is rebellious, then fast. If your relationship isn't working out, then fast. If you need financial assistance, deliverance, or healing to be restored, then fast!

Every year I fast once a week for the entire year. One day out of every week is dedicated to God. I have been on a 50 day fast and I have fasted for a full 30-day straight excursion. I am not telling you this to boast or brag, but I am telling you this to let you know that it can be done. I am telling you this to encourage you. I can't lie to you and tell you that I have gotten everything that I have asked for, but

I am going to continue to fast until I get everything that I desire. At times, my body gets weak and tired. I keep going because I refuse to give up. I am not one to lay down like a sick or like a wounded dog. I know that if I want something great to happen, then I have to do wonderful things or make great sacrifices. I must have some "get up and go" about myself. I must have a strong drive to complete the mission that I am set out for. I must be dedicated, determined, and disciplined. I can't afford to let another person think for me or decide what is best for me. I am not set out to please or impress anyone.

Truthfully, I love fasting. When I fast, I often hear directly from God. Fasting is a sure way to find out who you really are in the Lord. If you want to know the plans that God has for your life then I encourage you to fast!

Chapter 8

Repentance

People have the wrong idea of what true repentance is. So, this chapter gives a broad clarification.

Acts 17:30
"And the times of this ignorance
God winked at; but now commandeth all men
everywhere to repent."

A lot of people mistake the word repent. Let me break it down for you. Repent does not mean to be sorry for your wrongful actions. To repent is not just about asking for forgiveness and then leaving it at that. Even though several people feel guilty once they know they have sinned, it is because of the conviction of the spirit that is inside of them. It's something like on cartoons when you see the two little men standing on people's shoulders; I assume that one is portrayed to be Satan and the other is made to be God. Well, that concept is true in a somewhat caricature type of way, but not necessarily reality in the image that they initiate it. I don't know about you, but I don't have two cherubs sitting on my shoulders to tell me the difference between right and wrong. What I do have is a conscious and a subconscious.

We all know what conscious is. It's the totality of one's thoughts and feelings. It's our awareness level, understanding, discernment, surety, and mindful thinking. Our subconscious is what a lot of people aren't familiar with. The subconscious takes the place of the conscious. A subconscious is like a program included into our mind which we do not have to think about, we just do. It is what is embedded into us to automatically do. It's like when we react or say something before we realize we said it.

According to Your Dictionary, it describes our subconscious as something occurring with little or no conscious perception on the part of the individual (Your Dictionary). Moreover, the conscious and conscience run hand and hand. Conscience is the ability of recognizing right and wrong in one's own conduct. You can choose. Conscience is mentioned many times in the tenth chapter of I Corinthians.

Ezekiel 18:21-23
"But if the wicked will turn from all his wicked
sins that he committed, and keep all my
statutes, and do that which is lawful and right,
he shall surely live, he shall not die.
All his transgressions that he hath committed,
they shall not be mentioned unto him:
in his righteousness that he hath done he shall
live. Have I any pleasure at all that the wicked
die? Saith the Lord God: and not that he should
return from his ways, and live?"

Guilt, concern, and the knowledge of good and
evil forces us to want to repent. It's a part of our
nature, but we don't quite grasp the true meaning
if it. Ponder!

If we really did know the genuine meaning of
repentance then sin wouldn't be repeated. The
world would be a much more wonderful place,
peace would be in every home, school, job,
military, church, and person. The list goes on and
on. However, sin is habitual because we haven't
captivated the dynamic understanding of what
modest repentance is. So, I will disclose it to you.

Pure repentance is the reshaping of your approach towards ramifications, circumstances, situations, and people.

Most of all, we should change our viewing patterns on the perception of sin. People confuse repenting with forgiveness all the time, but repenting is *not* the same as forgiving. I asked two friends what they thought the meaning of repentance was. One of them thought that repentance was not just asking God to forgive you, but truly acknowledging your sin and letting whomever know you understand the error of your ways. The other friend thought that repenting was a person feeling wrong of what they were doing and wants to whole-heartedly turn away from their past ways. They are correct in certain instances. Just to be straight-forward, repentance is an application for modifying our behavior.

II Peter 3:9

"The Lord is not slack concerning his promise,
as some men count slackness;
but is longsuffering to us-ward,
not willing that any should perish,
but that all should come to repentance."
The Lord wants more than anything for us to

repent and be saved. What profit does God have for us to perish? However, if we don't repent, there will be consequences and repercussions. The book of Revelation describes all the torments and terrors that will be issued out by the just God. Are we willing to pay the price for our qualms? That is the question we must ask ourselves.

If you are still unaware of how to be penitent, James 4:7-10 gives a wonderful explanation.

It reads,

"Submit yourselves therefore to God, resist the devil, and he will flee from you. Draw nigh to God, and he will draw nigh to you. Cleanse your hands, ye sinners; and purify your hearts, ye double minded. Be afflicted, and mourn, and weep; let your laughter be turned to mourning, and your joy to heaviness. Humble yourselves in the sight of the Lord, and he shall lift you up."

We must also confess our sins and be baptized. After we have made an atonement with God, all of our wrong doings will be blotted out. We will no longer have to let our conscious sear us like a hot iron. The crimes and evil that we once committed do not exist anymore in the eyes of God (Acts 3:19). We are wiped clean as a sleight.

Our lives were filthy and gritty, but will appear white as snow to the Creator. So, don't believe for a second that there aren't any benefits for repenting.

II Corinthians 7:9
"Now I rejoice, not that ye were made sorry,
but that ye sorrowed to repentance;
for ye were made sorry after a godly manner,
that ye might receive damage by us in nothing."

If any man is wondering why his or her life is going haywire, it's because a work within you needs to be analyzed. It is like a mother who has a toddler that is crawling around the house in diapers. As bad as she knows that her child shouldn't touch the hot iron, that child still reaches out and touches the hot iron. When you are right there beside your child, you can stop them at every attempt. However, one day you may not be around or make it too late to stop them from touching it.

One day the child will touch the hot iron and learn a very valuable lesson. You may rejoice after that child has learned, but the fear of the experience dreads you. Just as toddlers must learn the what not to do, so do we, however, our lesson learning is on a higher scale.

That's why verse ten quotes *"For godly sorrow worketh repentance to salvation not to be repented of; but the sorrow of the world worketh death"*(II Corinthians 7:10).

Our trials and tribulations are for our mindset to be evolved into a righteous order. We go through what needs to for change. Believe it or not, did you know that God will change His mind? Yes, what I am saying is that God himself repents, but what we must keep in mind is that repent means to change your way of thinking.

God says in the book of Jeremiah 18:10, *"If it does evil in my sight, that it obey not my voice, then I will repent of the good, wherewith I said would benefit them."* Therefore, our prophecies don't come forward or they are held back. This is why the promises in the Holy Bible aren't fully manifested into lives. It is because God has repented or "changed His mind" about blessing you with a miracle because of your disobedience to Him.

Chapter 9

Names

Names are way more than what we actually think they are.

Proverbs 22:1
"A good name is rather to be
 chosen than great riches,
and loving favour rather than silver and gold."

What is a name? A name is a word or group of letters that gives recognition to a person, place, or thing. Humans don't like to be called out of their name. They desire to be called by their chosen name for acknowledgment. What amazes me is how a name effects and affects people. A human can be sound asleep—you could speak a thousand different words over them, but calling out their name is sometimes the only word that will awake them. You could be traveling through a busy bus station, airport, or during a parade. Even though there are many distractions and plenty of noise, someone calling out your name will allow you to locate them, despite all the traffic and noise.

Just to show you how powerful a name is, even a dog interacts with the name that you have given him. If the dog hears its name three blocks away from you, it will run to you. Names are how we set apart one individual from another.

If there is two people that look alike and you say, "Hey you," they wouldn't really know who you were referring to. However, if you call them specifically by their name, the other person wouldn't have to figure out whose attention you were attempting to gain. Another thing about a name is that it is labeled as a word or words by which any entity is designated.

Names are very wonderful because they carry a meaning. That's why it is very wise to be careful in choosing the name that you decide for your child. The name that you chose for your child is so dynamic that it intertwines with the destiny for their life.

If you think about it, most celebrities have names that just sounds like they were created to be famous such as, Bill Gates, Oprah Winfrey, Michael Jordan, Michael Jackson, and Steven Segall. Whether you know it or not, behind every name is a definition of character. Mary or Maryam means sorrow. Angel, Angie, and Angela literally means Angel (good or bad). Most of the people that have named their child Mary didn't even know that they had set forth sorrow for that seed.

Now let's take my name for example. Rahsaan means "child of God" in one language but in another, it means "future". My middle name is Aki, which means brother in Arabic, but in Greek, it means "laughter". My dad has told me that Aki means destination under another tongue, however, I have yet to unravel that. Some people get called terrible things because of their name. They may get laughed at or picked on because of the name that their parents gave them. That's why I advise you to use strong caution when deciding. The name that you pick for your loved one could cause him or her to have low self-esteem. On the flip side of things, people can also gain respect by the name give to them. It may sound cool enough that several people want to be around them. A name can cause you to have much manifestation and therefore build up a mighty character, but naming a person a name without knowing the definition of it is like saying a word that you don't know the meaning of.

Genesis 17:5
"Neither shall thy name anymore be called Abram, but thy name shall be Abraham;
for a father of many nations I made thee."

Even in the older days, God showed how significant a name was. Some people are so much more than their current title. The name that they have does not fit them. It holds them back from fulfilling the tasks, goals, and dreams that they are set out to do. I suppose that is why in today's time people get their name changed through legal registration. My mom once told me that it's not about what people call you but it is what you answer to that matters.

People are going to call you a lot of things (especially behind your back). However, you have to know not to respond to degrading names or even a name that's higher than your calling. You can't answer to a maintenance man's name if you are a chef. It just doesn't fit. That is why God changed Abram's name to Abraham, Sarai's name to Sarah, and Jacob's name to Israel.

I encourage and challenge you to search for the meanings of your names today. Some will find inner peace while others will know of the struggles they've been through. Thus, it is good to discover the depths of your name. Behind it may bring enlightenment to you.

Our Creator is a God of many names.

It may be pronounced differently depending on what ethnicity you are. Yet, it means the same thing in most cases.

Below are names with the translations for the Most High:

I Am That I Am – God will be what you need him to be.
Jehovah Jireh – The Lord will provider.
Jehovah Rapha – The Lord who heals.
Jehovah Nissi – The Lord our Banner.
Jehovah M'Kaddesh – The Lord who sanctifies
Jehovah Shalom – The Lord our Peace.
Elohim – Lord of Host.
El Roi – God of seeking.
Jehovah Tsidekenu – The Lord our Righteous.
Abba – The Lord our Father

We even call God a Rock, Deliverer, Judge, King, Holy One, Sheppard, Light, Redeemer, and Creator. Let me show you how powerful a name is. Acts 2:21 says, *"And it shall come to pass, that whosoever shall call on the name of the Lord shall be saved."* Our salvation is based upon our final destination in the afterlife, which is heaven or hell, which is solely based upon a name. Even the things that we go through living life on earth, whether good or bad, is based upon a name.

A lot of unbelievers may not believe, but the believers know how powerful the name of Jesus is. Just by the sound of Jesus' name, demons begin to tremble. Addictions are broken.

Poverty is ceased and curses are reversed. People are healed.

Have you ever wondered why everybody and everything has a name to it? When a baby is first born, the first question most people want to know is the child's name. Or if you ever had something fatal happen to you, the first question that is asked when you awake is your name. When you first met your spouse, you yearned deeply to know what his or her name was. Even inventions have names.

You can make something as small as a food dish to something as large as electronics. Whatever you create, you desire to give it a name. That is because names give significance, substance, and quality that makes it meaningful.

Chapter 10

Prayer

Communication is important in every relationship. So, prayer is having a one on one with your father.

P – **Pursuing** the will of God.

R – **Releasing** all our cares to Him, for He cares for us.

A – **Accessing** the presence of God.

Y – **Yearning** to learn more and more everyday

E – **Entering** to a place of peace and rest for your soul.

R – **Remembering** to seek His face, find Him, and witness His power.

Some of us don't know how valuable our prayer life is. We can be on the right track with God, then suddenly, our intimacy slips away. Prayer is basically communicating with a higher power. If you don't understand how to pray, just talk to God as if you and any other respectable individual would converse. Remember that God made you, so he knows and understands you. All that is required from the

Most High is that you try each day until you are at your best and highest peak. Nothing can be accomplished without you at least making an effort. You may not always be one of the greatest, but you will have some knowledge and experience of the matter. You don't have to be shy, ashamed, or afraid. God understands slang, monosyllables, sign language, mumbling, and overly aggressive wordings. Nothing can get past the Most High. If He understands speaking in tongues and dialects that are unknown to humans, then of course He can be familiar with your voice and style.

Some people believe that they shouldn't pray because they are not right with God or not where they should be in life. I am here to tell you that you should start somewhere. Have you ever heard that the longest journey begins with a single step? That is true in so many instances. How can you say that you are not right with God or where you need to be in life, when the word says for you to come as you are? Those excuses that you are using is a trick set up by the devil to deviate you from getting on the right track with God.

The enemy does not want to see you praying on your knees or bowing your head to someone who is greater. So, he discourages you from getting on your knees and praying to the Almighty One. He uses all types of tactics.

Prayer is the most imperative conversation that there is to have.

If you don't pray sometime during the day, then the rest of your conversations are in vain. To me, prayer can be considered as jewels, gems, and blocks of gold that are stored in my spiritual bank. It can and will be used as revenue for expenses and liabilities when needed.

Matthew 26:44
"And he left them,
and went away again,
and prayed the third time,
saying the same words."

The thing that gets to me the most is when people say pray and leave it alone. I am here to tell you today that they are wrong. Fair enough that when you pray and leave it alone, it could be considered as an act of faith. Yet, let's not forget that faith without works is dead. Praying is the most positive deed that one can do. Praying is a form of work. As a matter of fact, when we pray, we are praying that something works. So, praying and then leaving it alone is like praying for a job and never filling out the application. Even when prophets pray for you, most of them lay hands on you or anoint you with oil. Even that is labor. What we should do is push our way through. Pushing involves some type of force, action, or movement. The same way that prayer has an acronym, push has an acronym also.

P – Pray
U – Until
S – Something
H – Happens

Jesus Christ returned to pray the same thing to His Father repeatedly. Paul said in 2 Corinthians 12:8 "For this thing I besought the Lord thrice, that it might depart from me." So, if these great people can be repetitive, then so can we. The key is to push until we get our breakthrough.

Matthew 6:5-8
*"And when thou prayest, thou shalt not be
as the hypocrites are: for they love to
pray standing in the synagogues and in the
corners of the streets, that they may be seen of
men. Verily I say unto you, they have their
reward. But thou, when thou prayest, enter into
thy closet, and when thou shut thy door, pray to
thy father which is in secret; and thy father which
seeth in secret shall reward thee openly. But
when ye pray, use not vain repetitions, as the
heathen do: For they think that they shall be
heard for their much speaking. Be not ye
therefore like unto them: for your father knoweth
what things ye have need of, before ye ask him."*

Prayer is not a show.

We are not putting on a performance. We shouldn't do this to have the spotlight. There is no director yelling lights, camera, action. At times, we may have an audience, but we are not praying to the audience, we are praying to God. No matter how big or small the audience may be, we have to keep in mind that we are only praying with the audience and/or for the audience. When the word says "Enter into thy closet," (Mathew 6:6) it basically says that we need to find a calm, still, and secluded area with little to no distractions to make our supplications. Most of all, we should make our own submission sincerely and whole-heartedly, holding nothing back. God knows what we are going to say before we speak a word. He just wants us to be humbled and respectful to do it.

Matthew 21:22
"And all things,
whatsoever ye shall ask in prayer,
believing, ye shall receive."

A lot of us don't believe what we are praying for. We pray merely because that is what we are told to do. No one ever taught the hands-on experience of the depth or heights when making requests. So, we petition God then hope, wish, and assume that we ought to receive what we have asked for. Dedication, discipline, nor determination is a part of entreaty.

To not believe is like buying a car at the dealership and leaving it at the dealership because you never learned how to drive it in the first place. It's like telling a person that you would do something for them, but in your heart, you knew you were never going to do it. These things don't intertwine with each other. Unbelief is questionable because it carries doubt and fear. God is not pleased with

His children feeling improbable and praying in vain. We must gird up our loins. Grow a backbone and be bold and powerful in our battle as a warrior. Why do you think that in the sixth chapter of Ephesians, we are instructed to put on the whole armor of God and that prayer is required? That's because we are in God's army and manifestation takes place with being protected and ready for war.

I remember working at a big-time car dealership. I thought I was a fast and adequate talker so I would approach the customers as such. I believed that I could persuade anyone into buying a car. I talked about how good and nice looking the car was, how much gas it would save them, and how long the warranty would last on the vehicle. Little did I know; their mind had already been set on other things before my presentation. I did this several times and a lot of customers left without buying anything.

Unknowingly, my manager had been watching me for weeks. He was very experienced. He came to me and said, "The thing about selling a car is not talking, but listening." After he made that statement, it dawned on me that I was trying to talk a person into what I wanted them to do rather than listening to what they actually wanted. Therefore, neither of our needs were met.

When we pray we can't do all the talking. We must also listen to the voice of the Lord. Our father may be trying to say something totally different than what we are wanting Him to say. When we do not listen we often do not get what we expect. When we petition, wait, and listen it creates a way for both ourselves and God to be satisfied.

Another reason why we don't get what we pray for is because we don't know what to ask for or how to ask for it. That is why many people speak in tongues and different languages to the Most High. Our spirit intercedes us with groaning and murmuring. When grieving, sometimes just our grunts are enough (Rom. 8:26-27). Sometimes, we pray wrong. God's word says that we don't have what we ask for because we pray amiss. Perhaps you are praying that God brings your husband to you.

However, you forgot that since the beginning of time that Eve was brought to Adam. Adam was not brought to Eve. So instead of asking your husband to come to you, maybe you ought to ask

God to lead you to your mate. Now, I am not saying that everything I have stated is accurate, but what I am saying is that we have to pray the Lord's will, not ours. Even Jesus asked God to let His will be done. To get a full manifestation, it must be God's will. In the Book of Mark, the author speaks of men saying unto a mountain, "Be thou removed, and be thou cast into a sea" (Mark 11:23). Now this mountain that is spoken of is symbolic for our problems and infirmities. Yet, the key here is still not to have doubt in our hearts.

Prayer is very powerful. There are many benefits of it. Luke 11:11-13 says, "If a son shall ask bread of any of you that is a father, will he give him a stone? Or if he asks a fish, will he for a fish give him a serpent? Or if he shall ask an egg, will he offer him a scorpion? If ye then, being evil, know how to give good gifts unto your children: how much more shall your heavenly father give the Holy Spirit to them that ask him?"

God wants to bless His children with what we ask for if it is aligned within His purpose. Yet, when we ask for a specific car, house, or person to be in our life but we never get it, we should pay more attention to the 13th verse. It is not always about materialism and fleshly gain with God. He wants your spirit to be in order. So why should we be mad, disappointed, or confused when we ask for something and don't get it. Once again, we should examine ourselves and our hearts to find out the reasons. If there is anyone that you don't know how to pray for, the Book of Psalms is filled with significant and lovely prayers. I encourage you to search the scriptures until you find a prayer that best suits you. Prayer does change things! Believe that!

Chapter 11

Prophecy

A lot of people fear prophecies and do not believe in them. This chapter helps enlighten you about proper prophecies. It is not a coincidence!

On September 11, 2015 at approximately 2:45pm, I know I heard the spirit say to me without a shadow of doubt, "My son, prophesy unto the people saying they are a jealous and naïve generation comforted by worldly things. How be it, when I come I will come at a force un-reckoned by people. Take my word and guard it heavily, for the time is now. The time is near. Oh, jealous generation; I am tired —ashamed of your faces. Harbor not the labor. Shake not the crop. For the time has come when all will be lost." Most of this prophecy I understand, and the rest I do not. I can take a guess at the part I don't get and attempt to make logic out of it, yet that wouldn't be wise. God hath chosen the foolish things of the world to confound the wise, and the weak things of the world to confound the things that are mighty (I Corinthians 1:27). So, making an endeavor at what is logical or rational is stupidity to the one who made sense in the first place. Therefore, we go so wrong with prophecies and prophesying. We speak and act on worldly knowledge instead of the Spirit. Therefore, we end up getting misled or misleading others. The prophecy that was given to me was spoken clearly. It touched my heart and made me shed a tear after I heard the Greatest Glory say that He is ashamed of our faces.

We are a jealous and naïve generation.

The majority of sin and crimes are attributed by envy. Some people that are in relationships don't really want the person that they are committed to, yet they stay around merely because they are so jealous to see that person with someone else. The word "haters" has become a prominent word used by every race, gender, and age. If you break down their definition of what they proclaim, a hater is will describe a jealous individual.

We are naïve because we are so easily tempted

and influenced to get out of character. We lose insight on what our main focus should be on and we are swiftly drawn away from the big picture by getting thrown off track and becoming unsophisticated. We are ignorant to Satan's devices. Some of us do not stand for something, so we end up falling for anything. The part of the prophecy that got to me the most was that we are comforted by worldly things like video games, television, cars, food, clothes, money, and other people. We no longer allow the Holy Spirit to uplift us. We don't look up to God for guidance, protection, provision, or joy. We would rather let the things of the world make us feel good and give us strength.

Our Lord says that when He comes, He will come in an aggressive way not even considered by people. That means that our mind has not fathomed or imagined His return. Some knowledge is too high for us to attain, so it has been un-reckoned. Not even less than a week after I received this prophecy, hundreds of houses were burned in California. Then a flood destroyed men's properties and people's homes. My heart went out for the lost of their properties and loved ones. I believe that it was only the beginning of what is to come. We should heavily take the Lord's word and guard it carefully.

A lot of prophecies are spoken in parables. It may be months or years before the true meaning is revealed to us. This is why we must pray, listen, and watch for the manifestation of the evolution. Even though it may tarry, it will surely come if all the steps are provided accordingly.

I am not going to portray as if I am a person that sees and hears from God at will or very much. That would be false documentation if I did. I rarely hear or see any prophecies. As a matter of fact, the times that I yearn or feel that I need to hear or see something, I don't. I am a man that has been prophesied to many times before. Also, I have heard and saw some prophecies for myself. However, they tarry and at times I have became worried. I am not a machine to the fact that I am immune to certain emotions. So, when my prophecies aren't coming forth speedily, I become as the average man and faint. Yet, I pick myself back up. When I first began getting messages to tell others, I withheld the information because I was so unsure. Unsure if it was the truth and unsure of how the person would accept the prophecy. That was the worst mistake I have ever made.

Blood of the alleged recipients were on my

hands because I could have sounded an alarm of danger, but I didn't. I withheld people from achieving and establishing by not speaking. As I grew older and became more mature, I noticed that it didn't matter what I thought or what I felt. The Lord's will must be done. Either I can do what I was made to do and be blessed or buck and be cursed.

I Corinthians 14:22
"...*but prophesying serveth*
not for them that believe not,
but for them which believe."

During a long-term period of fasting, a lady had asked me if I had a word for her from God. This was odd because she knew that I was just stepping into my calling and had not yet fully adjusted. I went on to say to her a few words to her. "Yes, I have a word for you. You have to resist temptation more and come out of your comfort zone." I waited momentarily for a response from her. After she gathered her thoughts she agreed. She told me that I was right and asked why I had not told her that before. I replied to her saying, "Because you never asked." After I got off the line with her, I started praising and worshiping God.

Moments later I went into a trance.

The Spirit took over my temple and I began to see and hear many things that day. I received a word for the people that are in my immediate family. The way that it took place was uncommon though. I was seen looking at myself in a visitation center. An older black lady was walking past me as if it were normal. I had never saw her before. It was put in me to ask her if she ever had pain in her side before. She admitted that she did. I told her that God wanted me to heal her, but only if she believed that God could heal her. She agreed. I walked towards her to touch the bottom of her side area that was near her hip. I assumed that she was healed immediately because of what happened next during my prophetic experience. I remind you that I was still in the Spirit.

I was looking at myself and as I was watching through God's eyes, I saw myself looking around the visitation center and I noticed many people looking at me. There were about 50 people or so, and I began to turn and look at the them.

I told them and I quote, "You people want prophecies, but I will not give you good prophecies. Why do you think you should have good prophecies when you are not good? I am sent to be a prophet of correction, but most of you don't like correction!"

While I was still in this trance, I saw my youngest sister stick out her hand and say, "Rahsaan, I want to be healed." I turned and looked at her and replied in a deep and stern voice, "Your time is not now! Come out of yourself, you mean and selfish girl." Then I turned to my birth mother and said, "You let people step over you. God is tired of it. He wants you to step up and speak up. You are throwing God's blessings away when he gives them to you. God said don't you see that He is blessing you?"

Afterwards, the vision jumped to my eldest sister and I said, "The most precious stone is found inside of an oyster, but do you know how it is to crack the shell?" It wasn't until a few days later until I received a prophetic word or insight for the rest of my siblings.

The word that was spoken concerning my middle sister was, "You think you're walking, but you're not even walking. You think you're talking, but you're not even talking. Why are you eating? Haven't you eaten? You are like a woman with 50 degrees, but you're not even using them!"

Finally, I began to wonder why I hadn't received anything referring to my only brother. I didn't understand why I wasn't given a word concerning him.

Unfortunately, a word never came about him. So, I searched deeper in the Spirit and that's where I received my insight. I saw him vividly. He was standing in the dark. The vision was like he was outside at night time in some familiar backyard. The Gospel instructed us not to lean onto our own understanding. People go so wrong using worldly knowledge or common sense to figure prophecies out when the best thing for us to do is seek God, be patient, and wait on a divine revelation of the truth. When we start guessing and thinking we know the mysteries of Jehovah on our own free will, we end up being misled, indirect, and totally thrown off balance.

Our expectations set us up for failure, discouragement, greed and disappointment. The ways of the world are clearly erroneous with God's ways and thoughts. You may be thinking our creator means one thing when in actually he has another course from which assumed. I have felt hopeless and confused and lost a lot of faith and about to give up because I believed in my own heart what I thought the prophecies meant from what people told me. I tried to use logic and rational thesis' and theories to put together what seems as if I was absolutely correct.

Not knowing that God says, "But the natural man received not the things of the spirit of God: For they are foolishness unto him; neither can he know them, because they are spiritually discerned." (I Corinthians 2:14)

People that are proclaiming to be so smart and believing in their rationality and logic are far from the target. Simplicity is not always the way either. Just think about how many times your predictions have failed! My God's foolishness is wiser than men and He causes the things, which are not, to bring to naught the things that are. So, putting your conclusions against God is futile. Therefore, I wait humbly for a profound understanding before I reveal the secrets of my heart. It took a little time to get the depths of my family's prophetic insights. Now that I have them, I will share them with you. My youngest sister's foresight came first, but I didn't tell her; I told my eldest sister.

Deep down inside I wanted to know if what I saw, heard, and felt was real. I didn't want to tell anybody that something was from the All Mighty Himself when it was not. However, Maria told me that I ought to be careful of how I choose my words when talking to Shonte. Shonte was a very stern individual and at times she would take things the wrong way. I couldn't believe that God was telling me to tell her that she was selfish. Shonte had never been a selfish person to me. She was freely giving.

Despite of my warnings and my feeling that what I was about to say wasn't right, I told her the prognostic exactly the way it was given to me. I had to lay aside my gut feeling. I couldn't be lenient or give it to her softly, but I had to speak things in the fashion that was given to me. Weeks later, Shonte came to me and insinuated that she didn't understand why God would say she was selfish as in withholding items back. Yet, she was selfish as in not giving her whole self to the Most High. Keeping information from people because you believe it is not appropriate is a sure way to have their blood on your hands. Prophesying isn't nice. You may ruin friendships at the time but the best friend to have is God.

My mother's prediction was simple, straight-forward, and blunt. God was tired of the people walking over her or the people that play her kindness for weakness. If you con an individual, you can bet your bottom dollar that the eye of the Lord is on you. You didn't just trick His child, but you also tried to trick Him. God uses people at times to bless you. People could offer my mother gifts, money, a break on life, or simply just spending time with herself and she would turn them down. God was merely letting her know that when He had people bless her, it was He Himself blessing her, even if it is just someone offering her peace of mind or taking a load off from work.

Maria's omen was short but powerful. Truthfully, I didn't know how hard the shell of an oyster was, but I did know that pearls were found inside of oysters. God was letting her know that she had something that was highly valuable inside of her, but it is hard to get to. She will not crack. She will not surrender nor submit to our Father God.

My middle-aged sister's divination was told to her by another apostle before I ever told her. When this happens, it is called confirmation from the Holy Spirit.

The word says, "Out of two or three witnesses shall every word be established" (2 Corinthians 13:1).

When someone else has prophesied the same thing to you it shall surely and or suddenly come to pass. There is nothing like an agreement. However, the foresight that was told to Bianca was letting her know that whatever she was doing was nothing compared to what God has in store for her. The things that she was saying was mediocre to the powerful words she would be speaking.

Unfortunately, the part of the divination that asked, "Why are you eating? Haven't you eaten already?", was not disclosed to me. I could not guess what it meant because man's vagueness is superficial. Trying to uncover something that has an iron cloud over it is impossible without a higher power.

My brother's prophetic insight was much more complicated because I didn't hear anything at all. I only saw him standing in the dark. What I did know instantly was that darkness represents evil. I knew that Mario was not saved at the time and he said that there was no help for him. I'm here to tell anyone that believes that there is no help for themselves that God has a solution to every problem or situation.

If God sees what we don't see, then you know He sees what we do see. What God let me see after I prayed for an understanding my big brother was that deep down inside, he wanted to come to the light. The problem was that he is afraid of what his friends would say or think of him.

That is our setback today. **We are more**

concerned of what other people think of us than we are of what God thinks of us.

Some friends will always let you down but God will be there to pick you up. People are going to talk about you whether you are doing good or bad.

Jesus Christ died (and rose again) over 2,000 years ago and they still talk negatively about Him. You better believe that Jesus can care less about the insults they must say about Him. So why should we care what man thinks once we are doing a righteous thing? Like I said before, I felt that my brother wanted to come out of the dark, but the other reason why he didn't was because of fear. There are several types of fear.

Most people believe that the number one fears are death, heights, poverty, or losing. Other people fear snakes, spiders, rats, or just other people. I believe the number one fear is fear of the unknown. People fear what they don't know. They fear what they are not used to. That is why a lot of people don't change or evolve to a greater being. My brother was afraid of what it would be like living in the light. However, I don't blame him. There is power on this side. You have to cut out things that you adore doing and let go of what you were used to if it upsets to the Most

High (I know it was for me).

When you let go, that void is filled with something more valuable and significant.

To explore the world of the unknown is a whole different life of its own. Try it!

I Corinthians 14:22
"Wherefore tongues are for a sign,
not them that believe,
but to them that believe not:
but prophesying serveth not for them that believe
not, but for them which believe."

A lot of people are not going to believe the prophecies that prophets utter unto them. They have been condemned with an unbelieving spirit, blinded spiritually, and whipped by the enemy. Every soul is not of God, but that doesn't mean that you don't tell them what God has put on your heart to reveal to them. There is no telling what may happen down the line. However, like the passage above puts it, prophecies serve the anointed believer.

A lot of people get discouraged when things don't happen when they want it to and how they want it to. Some may even act like a spoiled kid and throw temper tantrums. In the Book of

Habakkuk its says, "For the vision is yet for an appointed time, but at the end it shall speak, and not lie: though it tarry, wait for it; because it will surely come, it will not tarry." (Habakkuk 2:3)

We must be patient and hold on to our faith. We must hold onto God's unchanging hand. If we begin to worry and waver then we will become like Peter when he began to sink into the water he walked on because he took his eyes off the Lord. It is mandatory that we stand firm on the promises of the Creator.

For Acts 1:7 reads, "It is not for you to know the times or the seasons, which the father hath put in his own power."

God only reveals to us what he wants to reveal to us. He is the commander and not us. I know that we have our own way of thinking things are supposed to go. But God has other plans sometimes. That is why I Corinthians 13:9 says, "For we know in part, and we prophesy in part." We cannot run nor can we hide from prophecies like Jonah did. They will always catch back up with us. God's word is tangible and ubiquitous, for He spoke in Isaiah 55:11, "So shall my word that goeth forth out of my mouth: it shall be accomplished that which I please, and it shall prosper in the thing where to I sent it."

By not submitting to God's word, havoc and chaos in your life will be multiplied. Have you wondered why dreadful things after bad things happen in your life? Or how about why nothing is going right or according to your plan? That is because being rebellious like Jonah will end up putting you into the belly of the beast. I remember once reading the story of Hezekiah. The king was sick unto death. Furthermore, a highly-respected prophet by the name Isaiah came to him and prophesied that he must set his house in order because he was about to die. However, the king humbled himself and turned towards the wall and prayed to God.

So, God demanded Isaiah to return to Hezekiah and prophesy unto him again saying that fifteen years had been added to his life because of his prayers.

This story made me wonder why prophecies fail or get reversed.

I know that God is not a man that He should lie, but He does change His mind. We were even warned of this in I Corinthians 13:8.

Now my next observation is why would prophecies fail? After all, prophecies are supposed to be mandatory, right? If you believe that all prophecies are mandatory then you are wrong.

Check out Hebrews 11:13. It says, "These all died in faith, not having received the promises, but having seen them afar off, and were persuaded of them, and embraced them, and confessed that they were strangers and pilgrims on earth." We don't receive our promises when we don't trust God, when we are disobedient, refuse correction, are not grateful, and when are not worthy.

Our blessings will be passed on to another person if we don't do what we are supposed to do. We must be prepared. The children of Israel's promises were passed on to numerous generations down the line because they chose to buck. Moses never made it to the promise land and he was the leader. Abraham only saw eight of his children birthed so he didn't understand how a nation that couldn't be multiplied came out of him. It reminds me of the verse earlier which says we prophecy in part and we know in part.

I'm about to close this chapter of prophecy. I hope and pray that you learn something very valuable. Before I end it, I want to leave an example on your mind from out of the book of Jeremiah in the Bible. The great prophet says in Jeremiah 5:25, "Your iniquities have turned away these things and your sins have withheld good things from you."

Chapter 12

Words

Whoever said sticks and stones may break my bones but words will never hurt must be confused, because sometimes words hurt more than any physical injury. Words cause emotional, social, mental, and spiritual stress and pain that may last longer than a broken bone.

James 3:2-8
"For on many things we offend all.
Of any man offend not in word,
the same is a perfect man,
and able to bridle the whole body.
Behold, we put bits in the horses' mouths,
that they may obey us; and we turn about
their whole body. Behold, also the ships,
which though they be so great, and are driven
of fierce winds, yet are they turned about with
a very small helm, withersoever the governor
listeth. Even so the tongues are a little

member, and boasteth great things.
Behold, how great a little fire kindleth!
And the tongue is a fire, a world of iniquity:
so is the tongue among our members,
that it defileth the whole body,
and setteth on fire the course of nature;
and it is set on fire of hell. For every kind of
beasts, and of birds, and of serpents, and of
things in the sea, is tamed, and hath been
tamed of mankind: But the tongue can no
man tame; it is an unruly evil, full of deadly
poison."

What are words? Today's society says that
words are a combination of sounds or letters that
symbolizes a meaning and that they are used to
express how you feel or what you think outside
of gestures. Words can be beneficial or critical.
I have seen people that get beat badly, but still
say things after the assailant has calmed down to
reinitiate the fight. Some people have had a gun
pointed directly to their head and the person that
had the gun decided if they wanted to pull the
trigger. Yet, the victim's words gave him that split
second conclusion to make up his mind. I have
heard of people that were on the verge of losing
their property or job, but they still could not hold

back the words that were fueling their tongue.

The choice of their selective statements determines the outcome of the matter. This planet was formed off the basis of words, for God spoke it and it came into existence. Before you and I were born, a conversation was first established between our mother and father. What I am attempting to show you is that death and life are in the power of the tongue (Proverbs 18:21). Words can cause you to be free of or in bondage. Words can decide your job, schooling, or marital status. The thing about words is that we must be careful about when and how we use them. The things we speak can help people as well as harm them.

Words are powerful and they mean a lot. What you say can determine how the next person lives the rest of their life. This is why Proverbs 18:4 says, "The words of a man's mouth are as deep waters." Whatever comes out of your mouth can be a blessing or a curse to another (James 3:10). I would prefer to bless people so I can end up getting blessed than to curse people and have a hex on my life. I remember reading once in the Bible where God tells His people that He will bless who blesses them then curse who curses them. That is why we must be cautious of how we put our mouths on God's children. Some people say and do things to others and are unaware that they are a child of God. Then they are wondering why all kinds of chaos and disappointments come into their lives. If we play with a child of God, then God is going to play with us. Speaking down and saying bad things will hold us accountable to pay the price (Jeremiah 30:16).

Sometimes, we even voice things that we really don't mean; we shoot the breeze,

"Hollywood talk", or utter sounds that have no significance to us.

I must bring to your attention that even the littlest things we say will be weighed.

Matthew 12:36 says. "But I say unto you that for every idle word men may speak, they will give account of it in the day of judgment."

This means that every time you open your mouth to merely say "hi" or "bye", you will be put on a scale in the last days. You may not think anything of what you speak, but God does. When I was younger, I was enrolled in an alternative school. Our punishment was to sit in class all day and write words out of a dictionary. Not only did we have to write the words, but we had to write down the definition before the day was completely over. I had close to 100 different words and definitions. Even though this was punishment, this class made me notice and like words. At first, I wasn't paying attention to the words or definitions. I was only writing them because I didn't want to get into any more trouble than I was already in. As I continued writing, I began to grow a passionate for the words and definitions. To pronounce the vast words was awkward at the beginning, but as I studied more, I started to speak eloquently. I noticed that most of the people I hung around weren't familiar with the language that I was speaking. People that taught the English language for years weren't aware of some of the immense words that I used. This is why I encourage people to expand their vocabulary. One word in a sentence can change the entire meaning of the subject. You may think someone is saying one thing when in reality they are saying something else.

It is not wise to let people talk over your head. One should always be willing to be up to par; ignorance is not excusable. If it is difficult for you to learn words, then you should be around people that speak them well so you can listen and learn. When you realize that big words are only an attachment from a little word, you will do good. For example, if somebody says, "I am

reluctant to un-disclose this information to you."
The average person may believe the person is
being polite or friendly. Contrary to your belief,
what he or she is really saying is that they don't
want to share any knowledge with you. You may
not be able to fully comprehend the terms. That
person will be able to talk circles around you all
day long. I am stating all of this just to say do not
be misled, but be willing to learn how to learn.

Usually when I feel my vocabulary isn't up
to par, I study words once a week or every day
depending on how much spare time I have.

People discover unfamiliar words all the time
so it is best to have knowledge. The greatest way
to memorize what you are studying is to say
or write the word repeatedly until it becomes
programmed into your brain. You can also use
the word throughout the day with different
people. Once you see that person that you've
word played with, normally the word that you
used with them will automatically register in your
mind whenever you see them again. Do not let
people deceive you with vain words (Ephesians
5:4). Some people do what is called a paradox
or oxymoron. They throw sounds and phrases
out hoping people will catch on to it. Sometimes
things they say have no substance, neither will it

symbolize anything. One thing that I do know is that the words of the wicked are to lie and wait for the blood, but the mouth of the upright shall deliver them (Proverbs 12:6). "Pleasant words are as a honey comb, sweet to the soul, and health to the bones." (Proverbs 16:23) Words can be tricky. They can be spelled the same but have a different pronunciation and meanings like "perfect" and "tear". Perfect can mean something or someone that is flawless or it can be used as an adjective to mean "complete." Tear can be a noun or verb. It can mean to rip something apart or can be described as a liquid that lubricates from the eyeball.

On the other hand, words can be pronounced differently and mean the same thing. Words spoken from a Southerner may sound different from a Northerner. A few words that have different pronunciations are words like syrup, envelope, tomato, potato, and some of our birth names. Just because someone says a word wrong to you does not mean it's wrong. It is only your opinion and opinions shouldn't be argued. "Turn" has one of the most separate meanings of any word and "if" is the greatest two letter word I know.

Chapter 13

Numbers

Numbers speak a language that if we listen and observe adequately we can interpret the symbolization of the dialect.

If we really think about it, numbers are everywhere. All that we do and say involves some type of number or should I say numerical system. Numbers help us rationalize and deal with things better. Without numbers, a lot of us would be confused and not organized. Back in the historic days, people were counting unknowingly. Things and people were accounted for with rocks or other substances. For every person or element, they placed a rock in its place before numbers came about. When we want more things in our lives we call it gain, but it is an *addition*. When we delete people out of our life, throw away appliances, or fire employees, it is then called subtraction. Even multiplying and division are a part of our everyday life.

Numbers have a major impact on our existence whether we notice it or not. The thing about numbers is that some people don't realize how important they are. This is why it is recorded that people suffer from that lack of knowledge. We can't understand what we are not aware of. Therefore, throughout the contents of this book, I will shine a light for many of you as well as confirm many mysteries.

Romans 1:20
"For since the creation of the world
his invisible attributes are clearly seen,
being understood by the things that are made,
even his eternal power and Godhead,
so that they are without excuse."

Have you ever wondered if numbers are symbolic—like each single, double, or triple digit represents something significant? It is natural to assume that the number 21 stands for maturity since the world only allows people that are 21 and older to enter casinos and buy alcohol legally. Seven is considered a lucky number and one means single. Five and six are affiliation numbers that are upheld by gang members and organizations. When the world says 100 or 1,000, that means full, whole, or refers to someone being dependent. However, numbers differ within the spiritual realm. The natural eye cannot envision spiritual things. The essence of numbers has separate meanings between what the world says they stand for and what they are. The world's lucky number seven means complete and perfection in the spirit. Twenty-one exceeds sinfulness, not sin. Five means grace and six means humanity. We all know that the number three represent the trinity of which God is; the Son, the Father, and the Holy Ghost. Jesus Christ also rose in three days. If you read your Bible carefully, you will notice the similarity in numbers. Jesus Christ fasted and spent 40 days and nights in the wilderness. Moses went on top of the mountain before he received the ten commandments for 40 days, and the children of Israel were trapped for 40 years. This is because 40 is a symbol or closing in defeat or victory.

Now what about the number seven? It is spoken of in revelation of the seven candlesticks, the seven beasts, the seven angels, the seven stars, and the seven churches. I have already given you the representation of the number seven in this chapter. Ironically, there are seven days in a week. Signs and wonders are all around us. We only should pay attention and believe. The time that you were born was specifically for you. Dates are arranged ethereally to manifest in the physical. Let's talk about a few examples of how numbers are interconnected with the world we know.

A deck of cards has four suits, which are intrinsic with four seasons. It has 52 cards, which are symbolic for the 52 weeks in a year. There are 12 tribes of Judah and 12 of Christ's disciples like the 12 months in a year. The earth is made up of one-third water, and so is the human body. Every inch of land, matter, and dimension is measured. We are identified by our height or our weight, which is also a numerical system. Even food is measured. Distance plays a major part in our mobility.

During the course of my unjustified incarceration, I noticed that every court day was involved around a family member's birthday or something related to my family's involvement like marriage or demise. Of course, the courts didn't know it because they weren't aware that they were merely being used as a pawn in a spiritual battle. One day I was involved in an altercation, and I was transferred to another barrack called the west wing. The interesting thing about this movement were the cells I entered. The first was cell number 14. I was aware of the number's meaning, but I immediately searched for the representation of the number 14 anyway. What stuck out to me was *bond slave* and *deliverance*. I thought to myself was this God's way of telling me that even though I was about go through a tough time, my deliverance was still in the way?

After a disciplinary hearing, I was moved to cell number 18. The number 18 meant judgment, to overcome, and captivity. Now, the reason I was admitted to solitary confinement was because I was accused of having a cellular phone in prison. A cellular phone is considered contraband, and we were not allowed to have them there. Yet, while I was thinking about doing time in the hole, a letter came to me from my lawyer. The U.S. courts agreed to hear an oral argument on my case. There was a catch. The date that they agreed to have the hearing on was also the 18th. Now was this a coincidence? Of course not.

Coincidences are for people with a lack of faith. You can only achieve as much as you believe.

The reason why this was not a coincidence was because of the confirmation in my next move. When I completed my time in those barracks I was moved to the 14th barracks. That place had over 21 barracks, but I was moved to the14th barrack like the number of the first cell I was in. The next part was mysterious. They moved me to cell number 18 in the 14th barracks. Wow! Now, the 14th barracks had 49 cells, but I was moved to number 18 just like the number of the cell I just came from. That was the date that a hearing on my freedom was given. The moral of this chapter is that you pay attention to dates, numbers, and time. It could be something miraculous happening in the spiritual realm. Have you ever noticed how a lot of godly people have divine encounters at 3:00 a.m.? This is also the time that

Jesus was said to walk on water. Signs and wonders are all around us. We have to be wise enough to watch out for it and not overlook the occurrences. At the same time, we must be aware that just like words, numbers can have many different meanings also. So, we must choose which interpretation of the number best fits us.

Interpretations of Numbers

One – Beginning, God, unity, first, rank order, new. (See Deuteronomy 6:4)

Two – Division, two becoming one, separate, judge, discern, agreement, witness, and union. (See Romans 9, Matthew 12:30, 13:32-39)

Three – Divine perfection, favor, the Trinity, deity, conform, obey, copy, likeness, imitate, tradition, completeness, perfect, testimony, and connected with the bodily resurrection of Christ and His people.

Four – Number of creation, the earth, four winds, four corners, reign, rule, kingdom, creation, unsaved, fleshly men, and boundaries.

Five – Grace, redemption, life, government, number of woman, atonement, the cross, works, service, bondage, taxes, prison, sin, and motion.
(See Exodus 13:18, I Samuel 17:40, Exodus 30:23-25)

Six – Number of man, the antichrist, the beast, Satan, flesh, humanity, carnal, idol, and manifestation of sin. (See Gen 1:31)

Seven –spiritual perfection, seven parables, seven days in a week, complete, finished, rest, and all. (See Gen. 2:2, Matthew 18:22)

Eight – New beginning, put–off, sanctification, reveal, manifest, resurrection, die, death, and new order of things.

Nine – Manifestation of the Holy Spirit, harvest, fruitfulness, fruition, fruit of the womb, finality, fullness, indicator, judgment, perfection, and divine completeness. (See I Corinthians 12:8-10)

Ten – Try or trial, test, temptation, law, judgment, government, order, restoration, responsibility, tithe, antichrist kingdom, and testimony.

Eleven – Mercy, end, finish, last stop, incompleteness, disorganization, disintegration, lawlessness, disorder, the antichrist, judgment.

Twelve – Joined, Holy city of God, governmental, perfection, fullness, apostolic, oversight, united, and governed.

Thirteen – Rebellion, backsliding, apostasy, revolution, rejection, double blessing, double cursing, and depravity.

Fourteen – Passover, deliverance, salvation, employee, bond-slave, servant, disciple, recreate, reproduce, and double.

Fifteen – Free, grace, liberty, sin covered, honor, and rest.

Sixteen – Free-spirited, without boundaries, without law, without sin, salvation, love, and sweet.

Seventeen – Spiritual order, incomplete, immature, undeveloped, childish, and victory.

Eighteen – Captivity, put-on, bondage, overcome, destruction, and judgment.

Nineteen – Ashamed, selflessness, without self-righteousness, faith, barren, repentant.

Twenty – Holy, tried, approved, wanting, and redemption.

Twenty-one – Exceedingly sinful.

Twenty-two – Light

Twenty-three – Death

Twenty-four – Priestly courses, governmental perfection.

Twenty-five – The forgiveness of sins.

Twenty-six – The gospel.

Twenty-seven – Preaching.

Twenty-eight – Eternal life.

Twenty-nine – Departure.

Thirty –Mourning, sorrow, consecration, maturity for ministry.
(See Numbers 20:29, Deuteronomy 34:8)

Thirty-two – Covenant.

Thirty-three – Promise.

Thirty-four – Naming of a son.

Thirty-five – Hope.

Thirty-six – Enemy.

Thirty-seven – The word of God.

Thirty-eight – Slavery.

Thirty-nine – Disease.

Forty – Probation, trial, testing, victorious, or defeated.
(See Jonah 3:4, Deuteronomy 8:2-5, Exodus 24:18)

Forty-two – The Lords advent to the earth, and Israel's oppression.

Forty-five – Preservation.

Fifty – Significance in fest, celebration and ceremonies, jubilee, freedom, liberty, Holy Spirit, Pentecost. (See Acts 2, Leviticus 25)

Sixty – Pride.

Sixty-six – Idol worship.

Seventy – Judgment, multitude, prior to increase, universality, Israel, and her restoration. (See numbers 11:10, Jeremiah 29:10)

Seventy-five – Separation, purification, and cleansing.

One-hundred – Solid, fullness, full measure, recompense, reward, God's election of grace, and children of promise.

One-hundred-nineteen – The resurrection day and Lord's day.

One-hundred-twenty – End of all flesh, beginning of life in the spirit, and divine period of probation.

One-hundred-forty-four – God's ultimate creation, redemption, and the spirit-guided life.

One-hundred-fifty-three – God's elect, revival, ingathering, harvest, and fruit bearing.

Two-hundred- Insufficiency.

Six-hundred – Warfare.

Six-hundred-sixty-six – Mark of the beast.

Eight-hundred-eighty-eight – The first resurrection saints.

One-thousand – Maturity, full stature, mature service, mature judgment, divine completeness, and the glory of God.

Chapter 14

Christians

"Go your way; behold, I send you out as lambs among wolves." (Luke 10:3)

First, just because an individual is labeled as a Christian does not mean that we are not going to have problems. I remember when I was a little boy. I used to hear my brother telling my mother that she had been praising God for years but she still had problems. He used to tell her that her children were bad, we were poor, and we still got sick. I often contemplated on the things he contested. I concluded back then that he was right. People still have trouble even though they are servants of God. Yet, I am here today to tell you that no one ever said that if you served God there wouldn't be trials and tribulations. Luke 10:3 lets us know that we will have attacks on our lives. Jesus Christ said that He will send us out as lambs among wolves. Do you not think that a wolf won't harm a lamb? The only way that sheep have any protection against predators is if the shepherd is present. If we read the Bible carefully, we will realize that everybody goes through troubling times. Job suffered affliction and he didn't do anything wrong.

The Israelites were God's chosen people, and they endured hardship. So, what makes a person think that just because someone is Christian they won't have difficulties? Jesus said that offenses will come! (Luke 17:1) As a matter of fact, when you are under the wings of the Heavenly Father, that is when the enemy comes at you even harder. Satan's job is to pry you out of God's arms. So, to pluck you away, he causes problems to make you second guess, doubt, and overthink a situation. Satan can trick us into thinking that God is not for us. He has even deceived a lot of people into believing that Christianity is something that someone made up to keep people from rebelling. Most say that being a Christian is only for the white folks. These are ridiculous myths to me. However, a person can only believe what they choose to. The biggest question for Christians to answer is why God allows babies to die? If there was really a God, then why do women get raped? Or why does sickness overtake us? I assume that we want Christ to help us, as if we are the ones in charge and not Him. Some-how we imagine Jehovah to pop up at the scene of every incident like the State Farm man on the television commercials. Well, that is not how the Most High operates!

Since the beginning of time, deaths, illnesses, and rape have taken place. If Cain would have never murdered Abel, then we would have never known the sincere heart of man. Men are filled with hatred, and the wickedness overtakes them and causes them to do these heinous acts. God allows these things to happen to show us that wickedness is in the world. However, we have the Holy Spirit to comfort us. We must remember that Lucifer has been declared as the prince of the universe. So, these unfair actions are under the authority of demons.

We have what I call *misplaced anger*. Instead of getting mad at God we should be getting mad at Satan because he is the initiator. Unfortunately, the critical point is that bad things aren't always directly aimed at the victim. Scary things happen to gain the attention of the ones surrounding the victim. It is supposed to draw us closer to God and not set us apart. Some people go the opposite direction, and most never recover. Instead of learning a lesson from the circumstance, we tend to only take the bad parts and run with them. No one is promised to live forever. No one is promised to go through life being unharmed.

We have guidelines and prayer to prevent these things, but some questions will only be answered at judgment day. Stop thinking that we are supposed to win every event, challenge, battle, and test. This is why Matthew 19:30 says, "But many who are first will be last, and the last first." Our father spreads His love around. What we are helped with, another may not be as blessed. What is best for another may not be what is best for us even though we may think that it is.

Acts 26:28
"And the disciples were first called Christians in Antioch."

A lot of us never pondered on where the word Christian came from. So, I will enlighten you. Back between the historic time of A.D. 47-49, Christianity was used as a mockery name to ridicule and discourage the followers of Christ. What we call Christians today was first named, "The Way" before accepting the name Christianity. It is like when someone calls you peanut head or junior since you were a child. At first, you abhor the name because you know people are calling you that as a joke. Yet, after so long, you accept the name and answer to is because perhaps you feel people will never stop calling you that name, or maybe it begins to sound catchy to you. Whatever the case may be, the name grows on you and becomes a part of your character. To be programmed into submission is not always a bad thing even though it could be susceptible. What started out as an insult has evolved for centuries. In other words, what was meant for our bad or to make us sad was turned around into something great!

Matthew 9:12 (NKJV)
"When Jesus heard that, he said to them, those who are well have no need of a physician, but those who are sick."

The thing that gets to me the most is how people judge Christians. I hear individuals all the time saying what Christians should and should not be doing. Or they will say how Christians should give them something all the time. They also judge the way we should talk and how we should feel. First of all, the Christianity status is between a person and God. No man on earth can put a limitation or expectation on a single human being because everyone makes mistakes. No one is completely flawless. This is why Jesus himself specified that if a person is not sick then they do not need a doctor.

Don't think for a minute that all Christians are the holiest of the holy.

Only one man is without sin and that is Jesus Christ. Even the word says no man is righteous, no, not one. So, we shouldn't be so quick to judge or put a label on anyone. Christianity is merely a lifestyle that people strive to perfect. We go through a lot and every day is a struggle. **We are not Jesus; we are human beings that make up the body of Christ called Christianity.** We are merely followers that have an example sought out for us. This does not necessarily mean that someone won't deviate from the course. If we don't get sidetracked or distracted from time to time, then we wouldn't be men or women, would we? We would be God.

Do not think that just because a person is a

Christian that they know everything about the Bible. It takes years to sufficiently and effectively study line upon line and precept upon precept of the Bible. Some people have problems with memorizing things and others have trouble reading. I have seen non-believers and other denominations debate with Christians to challenge their Christianity by their knowledge. Again, I cannot say it enough, the Christianity status is between God and that person. God judges by heart and intentions. Man cannot see the heart or someone's true intentions, and they cannot proficiently judge the next person or act as if they are an expert in value or something. They must not know that James 3:2 says, "For we all stumble in many things."

John 14:6
"Jesus said to him, "I am the way, the truth and the life. No one comes to the father except through me."

Jesus Christ is the intercessor for Christians.

It is like when people have a wing guy or middle man in business transactions and such. It is like a chain of commands in the military. No one is permitted to go straight to the lieutenant unless they've gone through the sergeant. No one can pass the major without consulting with the captain. If they bypass, they have broken the chain of command. After Elohim destroyed the people on earth by water in Noah's day, the people were still rebellious. God was fed up. He was going to do away with the earth because the offering of animals was not longer savory to God.

The ultimate lamb was sacrificed which was Jesus Christ. People no longer went through priests or continued to offer up animals. We were cleansed through the blood of Jesus. We must go through Jesus to get to God. Therefore, since we are naturally corrupt and evil minded, God looks at us through the blood of His son. Christians are to pray in Jesus' name. If we break the chain of command then we are wrong.

Hebrews 13-1:3
"Let brotherly love continue.
Do not forget to entertain strangers,
for by doing some have unwittingly
entertained angels. Remember the prisoners
as if chained with them – those who are
mistreated – since you yourselves are in the
body also."

Now, don't get me wrong, Christians have rules, commandments, and instructions that are designed to abide by. The instructions and correction of the Bible is what is established or measured as a Christian even though the entire scripture is the fulfillment. I have highlighted verses accordingly. The way of Christians is outlined in Luke 6:32-45 and the entire chapter of Proverbs 3. How Christians are to act is briefly described in Ephesians 5:1-21 (NKJV) and Ephesians 4:32 (NKJV). To define a Christian is stated in Matthew 5:3-16 and Luke 14:26-33. Also, refer to Acts 26:28 and I Peter 4:16.

The above scriptures are for you to identify yourself and/or others as a Christian or how to become a Christian if you aren't already. However, one thing that we must remember is that we are a workmanship and we only draw to Christ if the Lord chooses to send us to Christ (John 6:44).

If God does not put it in our spirit to be Christians then we will not be a Christian. With if the Spirit leads you to use the Bible scriptures I gave you, please do it willingly and speedily. If nothing has caught your attention by now in this book, just keep reading. I'm sure something will attract your attention.

Chapter 15

Salvation

Salvation is not all about being holy and sanctified. It is about knowing what you are saved from. Yet, once you've become saved, it is your responsibility to do the right thing, because you are now bought with a price.

Matthew 25:41-46

"Then he will say to those on the left hand, depart from me, you cursed, into the everlasting fire prepared for the devil and his angels. For I was hungry and you gave me no food; I was thirsty and you gave me no drink; I was a stranger and you did not take me in, naked and you did not clothe me, sick and in prison and you did not visit me. Then they also will answer him saying, 'Lord when did we see you hungry or thirsty or naked or sick and in prison, and did not minister to you?' Then he will answer them saying, 'Assuredly, I say to you, in as much as you did not do it to one of the least of these, you did not do it to me.' And these will go away into everlasting punishment, but the righteous into eternal life."

In order to be saved, we must first know what we are being saved from.

It is like when a toddler first reaches out to touch a stove, iron, or furnace. The child does not know the effects of it until the child experiences it. Once the child has experienced what touching something very hot feels like, the child learns to never do it again. However, if the child never touches it, then the knowledge would never be obtained. This is the very reason why some mother's intentionally have their child graze the hot surface. They don't do this to be mean, but to teach the child what not to do. In other words, they are showing the child what they need to be saved from. If they don't intentionally do it, then the lesson may be learned in a more terrible way.

God allows tragedies to happen to us and people around us to teach us what we are being saved from. Salvation is vital because above all we are being saved from the forever burning flames of hell.

The author of Acts says, "We must through many tribulations enter the kingdom." (Acts 14:22). To enter true paradise and true euphoria takes a lot of endurance. It is not a comfortable ride to reside by the Father if all creation. I assume this is why God is often nicknamed *mother nature* because He is so caring and associated with a loving mother.

It is noteworthy to look at the first few lives of the above passage. What caught my attention the most is where our Lord would quote, "Depart from me, you cursed, into everlasting fire prepared for the devil and his angels." (Mathew 25:31-46) The last part says, "Go away into everlasting punishment, but the righteous into eternal life." You see, a lot of us want salvation but we aren't doing what's required to acquire complete salvation. A lot of people are quick to judge a homeless person or drug addict.

If someone below their standards needs to be fed or is thirsty, then they will deny that person food or water. Perhaps they believe the person will use their money for things other than food, but you don't have to necessarily give them money. You can buy the food and water for them and hand it over personally. Others don't want to help people that are sick or without clothes because they feel that if it's not them suffering then everything is okay. Some think that if they are around a person with AIDS, HIV, herpes, or any other contagious virus that they can contract the virus by air or by touching them which I understand. However, the thing that gets me the most is when Jesus said He was in prison, but no one came to see Him.

Ironically, I was listening to a show on the radio one day and on this show they held a census and it totaled out that eighty percent of the people were against prisoners. They didn't know any of the prisoners, yet still hated them. They didn't know if some had been falsely accused, if they've learned their lesson and repented, or if they have already paid for their crime. They were judged by believers and non-believers of the word. It is clearly written in Matthew 25:41-46 that these same people that don't do service for the needy, neglected, and rejected will be the ones burning in hell. How does anyone expect to be delivered in the last days when it is in their power to save or minister to someone else, but they turn down the opportunity?

Jesus Christ says if done to the "least of these", then you have done it also to Him. Our burdens and yokes have been cast upon the cross. So, the people that look at strangers awkwardly, deny food, drink, clothes, and refuse to treat someone in prison kindly will be told by our Lord to get away from His presence because they are a worker of iniquity.

Acts 2:21
"And it shall come to pass that whoever calls on the name of the Lord shall be saved."

As we should know by now, salvation literally means to be delivered, redeemed or saved from the plagues that are written in revelation. My mom always told me that salvation is free, but we pay a price for the anointing. God gives us protection freely if we are willing to accept it.

Salvation is not hard to attain. Salvation is very easy.

We don't have to assume that it is complicated. Acts 2:21 gives the step to salvation, and that is calling on the name of the Lord. Yes! It is as simple as that! Simply call on the name of the Lord and if you believe with your heart that Jesus is the son of God, then you automatically have salvation. Now the next step is characterized in Luke 10:25-28 which says, "And behold, a certain lawyer stood up and tested him saying, 'Teacher what shall I do to inherent eternal life?' He said to him, 'What is written in the law? What is your reading of it?' So he answered Him and said. 'You shall love the Lord your God with all your heart, with all your soul, with all your strength, and with all your mind, and your neighbor as yourself.'

And He said to him, 'You have answered rightly; do this and you will live.' If we as people in today's era live accordingly to Acts 2:21 and Luke 10:27, then we will not be in danger of hell's fire. As long as we are in line with the scripture then we will surely live. We don't have to worry about flesh, nor Satan deceiving us as if we will burn in hell along with them. We are emancipated from sin.

Chapter 16

Religion

We must remember that religious leaders killed Jesus over religion!

James 1:26 (NKJV)
"If anyone among you thinks he is religious, and does not bridle his tongue but deceives his own heart, this one's religion is useless."

Religion, as the world puts it, is an organized system of beliefs and rituals centering on a supernatural being or beings. Religion can also be labeled as a dogma or strict doctrine to abide by. Religion, as the contemporary world puts it, has been taken far out of context from the original meaning of what God initially intended it to be. There are over a thousand different religions today. Men have made up their own because they believe that something should go this way or that way.

Perhaps they felt that something was awry with what they have been taught all of their lives, so they take it upon themselves to change and fix things how they see fit. How devastating is it that many different cults and denominations are taken from the root? God only proposed one religion and one religion is supposed to be through us all. Yet, opinions have defeated this purpose because of an un-answering yet complex rationalization.

When men begin to utilize worldly wisdom, knowledge, and understanding, division comes about. Where there is division in a house, organization, or religion, they will slowly split up or get ripped apart. It is somewhat like branches falling from a tree. Now everyone and everything are governed by something whether they realize it or not. There is nothing without rules, regulations, standards, morals, commandments, or instructions. There is a specific way that one is expected to present themselves. The essence of the presentation when presenting yourself has somehow become vague or rather misleading.

Today, people display themselves as how they assume others want them to be or they attempt to keep up with the trends and styles. Even their religion has a fashion statement to it. If a woman does not wear a long dress or a man does not wear a bow tie then they are out of order, as some critics would put it. They act as if clothing can save their soul or that they can only be accepted into paradise with their made-up dress code, not knowing that there is only one supreme being that we need to prove anything to. That is why it is written in Timothy, "Be diligent to present yourself approved to God, a worker who does not need to be ashamed, rightly dividing the word of truth." (II Timothy 2:15 NIV). The thing that baffles me is how religious people let anything come out of their mouths. Their tongues are a breathing flame with venomous poison—speaking of things that they have no knowledge of. Yet, the things that they do have knowledge of should be kept silently to themselves if it is 100% malarkey. Ambivalence, gossip, cursing, and hurtful words are open like a furnace that is turned up to the max. They disregard that God says, "But shun profane and idle babblings, for they will increase to more ungodliness." (II Timothy 2:16 NKJV) I was once in the presence of a highly self-proclaimed religious brother.

At the expense of his entertainment he told me that it was okay to masturbate, curse, lust, and have evil thoughts because we are human and God understands. I disagreed with him. Even though I have issues of my own that I cannot control and sometimes fall weak from time to time, I am not sick-minded enough to say that it is okay. I Thessalonians 4:3 tells us, "For this is the will of God, your sanctification to abstain from fornication." Lord knows He blessed us with the ten commandments. So, to say that God understands something that He specifically ordered us not to do is plainly an excuse to do what you want to do and not feel guilty about it.

Covering up your motives is not a way to justify your actions and/or attitude about things. People are confused and misled as to what true religion is. It is hard to win sinners over when they are on the outside looking in and seeing no difference within our lifestyles. The religious and the sinners are on the same level so they wonder what would be the sole purpose of converting.

James 1:27
"Pure and undefiled religion before
God and the Father is this; to visit orphans and widows in there,
and to keep oneself unspotted from the world."

I can go without saying that I have no religion. Religion defined today is the ultimate display of misrepresentation. Let's take a view at the outlook. Christians are against Christians. Muslims are against Muslims. Jews are against Jews. What do we have here? Religion as the world puts it separates God's children. It was once said that every denomination or non-denomination were just different roads that people took, but they all lead to the same God. Whether this is true or not, you must search your own heart and be unbiased with the decision you make. However,

I don't concur with the feuding. A Pentecostal church can look at themselves as if they are more righteous than a Baptist. The Baptist may look down on the Church of God in Christ. The Catholics believe their ways are better than Jehovah witnesses and so on. The odd part is that all of them claim themselves to be Christians. It is a disgrace how religious people can act. At times, I wonder if these cults or religions are like a gang such as the Crips or Bloods warring with each other. Even if they are not fighting physically, they are fighting mentally, spiritually and socially. The Muslims are not excluded. Neither are Rastafarians, Atheists, Hindu, or Jews. Do you see how Sunni Muslims fight with the Nation of Islam? But the Nation of Islam say's that their ways are different from other Muslims. Al-Qaida and Isis are against everyone. On the other hand, Christians turn their noses up at Muslims. Muslims do not respect Christians.

The house of God has sectioned themselves off far from communicating with others and therefore act as if they are better than the next person. Well, I am a man and I'm not going to bite my tongue. All religions will be called out in this book. As a matter of fact, while I am speaking my mind, it is my belief that the biggest war of all time will be the Muslims and Christians. If I'm not mistaking, this war may be what brings the world to an end.

To let the truth be told, in a comparison Muslims have more discipline, dedication, and determination than Christians, Jews or any other Religion that are amongst us. They also have more knowledge of themselves, God, and their religion. Don't get me wrong, I am not condoning, commending, or condemning anyone. I am merely giving credit where credit is due.

I have been around many kinds of people. I've notice that even in psychology, philosophy, politics, physics, and a variety of organizations are more equipped with education. Muslims are also more serious about their beliefs than any other religion. Why do you believe they are willing to blow themselves up with bombs and leave their family behind? I'm not saying that other religions aren't educated, determined, serious, or don't have discipline. I know many Christians that are devoted to their studies and are highly intelligent. I am merely speaking from observation and experience rather than theory and speculation.

I grew up in a Christian home and saw that every religion had people who loved God to fullest. However, when you compare the religions, you tend to find out things that you normally wouldn't if you only viewed intrinsically.

Chapter 17

Holy Bible

What is the true meaning of the Holy Bible? What is it for and to whom was it written to? Should I believe the words therein? Are the scriptures watered down?

H – He
O – Only
L – Left
Y – You

B – Basic
I – Instructions
B – Before
L – Leaving
E – Earth

If you think about it, Jesus did leave us basic instructions before leaving earth. The comforter came after His death. However, before Jesus' demise he gave us parables, directions, and teachings. The Bible does not give us a second by second manual as if we are robots that are programmed. It gives us some insight on how we ought to live our lives. The reason I say basic instructions is because it gives you the fundamental components of living life, but not the depth of it.

A lot of things we must learn through experience or let the spiritual elders and the Holy Ghost teach us. Let me give you an example so that you can fully understand what I am saying. For instance, we all know that one day each one of us will witness death unless we are the ones included in the rapture. However, the Bible does not specifically tell us how we are going to die. Another example is that Jesus warns us that offenses will come against us. Yet, the word is filled with some type of offenses, but several them are omitted.

Perhaps your offense could be a plane crash, people calling you names, a tumor, or a car wreck. The next and final example is that the scriptures tell us that God will give us a way to escape temptation, but it failed to mention every route. Maybe your spouse steers you the right way. Your job, your hobbies, or something essential occupies your mind.

The basics are to inspire you and give you aspirations. They convey what to look out for and what to look forward to. It is the start of life and knowledge, for one must plant a seed before it is able to grow. Details are there to develop you and help you grow.

The Holy Bible has many mysteries, ministries, and rumors. I have heard of missing books. The prominent one is the book of Enoch. Now I have never read any chapter from the book of Enoch, but the few who have read it have told me it was powerful. I am not in position to officiate whether the book came out of the Bible or was intentionally kept secret. However, I do believe that there were many scribes that were written around Jesus' time that we have not heard of. Perhaps the 66 chapters that are documented are all that God felt was needed for today's time, understanding that too much information can turn a person crazy or just confused (which is why certain scientists go mad).

There is something that I would like to bring to your attention. Read Joshua 10:13. You will discover that the Holy Bible itself reveals a book called Jasher that is not included in today's Bible. Joshua 10:13 (NKJV) says, "So the sun stood still, and the moon stopped, till the people had revenge upon their enemies. Is this not written in the Book of Jasher? So, the sun stood still amid heaven and did not hasten to go down for an entire day." The Bible itself gives you evidence that there are books missing because if you scan through the scriptures you can't find the book of Jasher. Joshua and the people that he was ministering to knew there was a book called Jasher. A lot of us today probably never heard of it.

Also, the author Samuel in the Bible knew that there was such a book called Jasher. II Samuel 1:18 (NKJV) says, "And he told them to teach the children of Judah the song of Bow, indeed it is written in the book of Jasher." Rumor has it that the Romans have concealed certain books out of the Bible for the sake of themselves. It is said that only the Pope and his selective few know of this secret. I believe that the Pope of Rome should be asked publicly of the existence of such scriptures. Knowledge is of no value if it isn't shared. For those who add or take away from the Bible, they must have never read of the dangers that will happen to them. Revelation 22:18-19 says, "If anyone adds to these things, God will add to him the plagues that are written in this book, and if anyone takes away from the words of the book of this prophecy, God shall take away from his part from the Book of Life, from the holy city, and from the things which are written in this book."

It hurt my heart when I heard that certain members from the gay community reformed the Bible to expediently suit their homosexuality. I couldn't believe when I saw the verses that condemn the acts of same sex were taken out. Preachers, deacons, and other church members add scriptures of what they want out of another person. They circumvent or enthrall with what is really written, then add extra spice or flavor of their own. All of this is manipulative and shrewd craftiness. Another mystery is of whom the Holy Bible was dedicated to. During the times of the Old testament, rarely anything was approved unless it came through the King or if it was for the King.

A lot of people may or may not have wanted the book dedicated to the King, but they may have saw that it was the only way to get it published. Before the Bible arrived in America, it was tribute to King James. There are accusations that King James was a homosexual. I'm not sure if this has been documented or not, but no one can be 100 percent sure because we weren't living to be a witness. I wouldn't put anything past anyone. If you take a few seconds to rationally think about the situations, would you believe the people from back then would allow a man to rule over them that was considered an abomination?

II Peter 1:20-21
"Knowing this first, that no prophecy
of scripture is of private interpretation.
For prophecy never came by the will
of man, but holy men of God spoke as they
were moved but the Holy Spirit."

People have debated and wondered about many different translations of the Bible. Truthfully, I have raised an eyebrow many a time myself. I believe that some individuals are so caught up in correct grammar and being politically correctthat they prefer to change the wordings to fit into their society. Old English, sentence fragments, or statements that do not have "correct" punctuation, verbs, adjectives, and nouns are forbidden to the m. How dare you speak of broken language in their home? Ebonics and passages that do not fit their sophisticated customs are a disgrace. They do not know that when they change the linguistics up, they take away the depth and the significance of the verse.

They intend to make the Bible easier to read and understand. They fail to realize that Jesus Christ Himself said, "To you it has been given to know the mysteries of the Kingdom of God, but to the rest it is given in parables, that seeing they may not see, and hearing they may not understand." (Luke 8:10). This may come as a shock, but everybody isn't supposed to understand the scriptures. Everyone is not of God, and if those who are not of God are able to interpret divine knowledge, they will use it in a wrongful way.

The way that the scriptures were originally written is the way that God intended for them to be done. I don't believe that the Most High asked anyone to change up anything. What isn't broken does not need to be fixed. When you try to fix something that isn't broken then you usually will end up breaking it.

Furthermore, when the word is advanced, it takes away from people asking God to give them the knowledge that is required! For it is written, "And he opened their understanding that they might comprehend the scripture." (Luke 24:45)

When a commentary is given then there is a lack of needing to meditate, soul search, or seek for that inner yearning. Just like scientists are playing God by cloning people, traveling to space, and disrupting the climate control, they are also playing with God changing the wording in the scriptures. I remember growing up in church. Back then, there was only one Bible that everyone read from and that was the King James version. It was not the NKJV, NIV, or any of the other versions that they have today.

When the preacher read from the King James version, we did not have to look at the sentences that are now changed. It was not about proper grammar or eloquent speaking. It was about the word of God and that was it! Then later came the Gideon's Bible, and now hundreds of other versions have been written. I'm not sure if people are doing this for the money, fame, or salvation. The Bible is the most sold book throughout the world. Publishing companies make millions of dollars off the book. Greedy people saw how successful it was to sell Bibles and began to make many different versions to gain their own piece of the pie. They don't care if it's worded differently or not, which is sad because many are misled and spiritually blinded. The Holy Spirit or someone led by the Holy Spirit is the one that was ordained to give you true meaning. Even the prophets whom wrote the Bible supplied their own solutions or explanations.

God was responsible by speaking through them and for them. Moses, Paul, nor any other uttered their own thoughts; everyone had doubt. Even I have had my escapades of doubt. Ramifications make us that way. It is human nature as a fleshly being to harbor doubt. How can we believe in what we haven't seen or experienced? I have been on the verge of thinking everything written in the Bible was a lie. A lot of situations just didn't add up. I read where it says, "The fervent pray of the righteous prevail." (James 5:16) Yet, when I became sincere and even when many saints showed deep feelings in their prayers to God for my circumstances, nothing changed. I'm aware the scriptures insinuated faith of a mustard seed can move mountains, but even through my faith, my problems still exist.

One thing I noticed is that the Bible is somewhat like a jig-saw puzzle. For it to be complete you must have all the pieces. Nothing can be missing. If you are lacking one component, then the fulfillment of the passage won't be activated. You can have all the faith in the world but if you aren't doing the work that is required then your faith is in vain. It's like praying for a job and never filling out an application. It's like quoting scriptures that you are healed from, and not believing them. It is also like pleading the blood over cancer and still smoking cigarettes and drinking alcohol. It just isn't going to work that way! For anything to operate effectively, one must be whole hearted and apply in the fullness and entirety of the matter. You can't say, "If I ask I shall receive," but do not follow His commandments. That is like expecting to receive a check from the bank worth a million dollars and you only put five bucks in your bank account.

Now the greatest myth of all time is the rumor that the Holy Bible was written for the slaves and the people that wrote it wanted to control the world with scare tactics. Some believed that it was written so that they could get people to turn the other cheek. The word is packed with humbleness and kindness. Letting people try treat you any kind of way creates opposition. The opposition can use the believers like puppets. FYI, a sizable percentage of slaves didn't know how to read. Slave owners forbid them from attempting to learn how to read. So, to say that the Bible was written for the slaves is absurd and borderline ludicrous. The funniest thing that I ever heard is that the Bible is the white man's book. Some say it was only written for Caucasians.

Unfortunately, I never knew that God saw color. For people to minimize and call a spirit prejudice is totally uncalled for. It is ridiculous to say one book is for the whites and another book is specifically for the blacks. If you thoroughly search the contents of the book, you will find out that God gives us a choice. Nothing in the scriptures is forced upon anyone. You must read and pay attention. Don't listen to opinions of others, but develop the truth for yourself by seeking. Read, review, then reflect upon what you read.

II Timothy 3:16-17
"All scripture is given by inspiration of God, and is profitable for doctrine, for reproof, for correction, for instruction in righteous that the man of God may be complete, thoroughly equipped for every good work."

How peculiar is it when people go against Jehovah's word? They scramble through the Bible and the Quran to find passages that fit themselves while skipping and rambling over pages until their flesh is satisfied. They search for sayings and ways to justify their wrong doing or sinful behavior, not reading the entire book only partial.

True enough, I believe in the Bible but I don't believe because someone else told me to believe in it. I don't believe in it because I feel that's what I am supposed to do since others around do. Whatever I choose to believe in, I believe it because of the conviction the word gives off when I read it. I believe because I feel the spirit erupting when I call on the name of Jesus. The experiences I have had caused me to see the truth in the word. I do not read the Quran or Catholic books because I get fully fed off the Holy Bible. I feel that the Quran and other books separate teachings from the Bible itself. One thing that I noticed is that most them that solely dedicate themselves to the Quran and Jewish books also read the Bible.

The Quran and other religious books may not be enough for them to get full of by itself. That is for them to decide. One thing that I am sure of is that the Bible doesn't need any other book to coincide with it. Every other book is written after the Bible and in accordance to the Bible. These other books were written close to 400 years after the Bible, so tell me who the originator is!

The 14th and 15th verse of II Timothy says, "But you must continue in the things which you have learned and been assured of, knowing from whom you have learned them and that from childhood you have known the Holy Scriptures, which are able to make you wise for salvation through faith which is Christ Jesus." A lot of people turn to different doctrines because they've prayed, and the things they prayed for didn't happen or they were let down somehow. They grew up knowing or hearing of the scriptures at least once in their lifetime, but never continued to seek further. Perhaps they didn't grow up in a faith-based home or somehow, they were converted to another religion. I have seen many people convert simply because the people around them did or they wanted to feel like a part of the crowd.

I am here to tell you that God is not concerned about you being down with homies or changing up to be with a woman or man. You are going about dogma the wrong way if you are. Have you noticed that philosophy books have phrases that come out of the Bible such as, "As a man thinketh." Even psychology, anthropology, and self-help books are written from things learned in the Bible.

Even the movies and television shows that we watch quote scriptures. Some of us are even unaware that the things we say in our everyday life are Biblical. I remember telling myself one day that I found specific things out about life the hard way. Even though experience is the best teacher, the word of God is even a greater teacher. Through living life, I found out how women, family, and friends are. I found out how the streets and enemies are. I learned the rough way about liars and how bosses and individuals with authority are.

Unfortunately, I found these things out the hardest way. It's a shame too because all I had to do was pick up the Bible and read it. The Bible has basically everything in it in life that we are going through. It talks about temptation, the wages of sin, family going against each other, relationships, friendships, deceitful woman and men, and so much more. What took me years to find out on my own, I could have learned in months. So, I encourage you to pick up the terrific book and read it before it's too late!

Chapter 18

Prophets

I must admit, talking about prophets is a scary subject for me. How can they see into my life? Is this some type of practice?

Matthew 10:41
"He who receives a prophet in the name of prophet shall receive a prophet's reward."

Some people believe that Elijah Muhammad was the last prophet that ever existed. They say that after Muhammad, there will be no more prophets. Unfortunately, these individuals do not know the true definition of the term. There are still seers and prophets today. A prophet is one that foresees an occurrence before it happens. I am not referring to Deja-Vu or neither do I believe in coincidences. You and I can be considered as a prophet if we with a divine inspiration. If you are a child of God, you are equipped with a gift, whether you know it or not. Just like our earthly father knows how to bless and flourish his children with gifts, our heavenly Father grants us gifts as well. It may take some time for us to fully develop skills for the gift, but it is instilled inside of us to do so.

Deep down in our inner being exists a magnificent present waiting to be opened. However, not all our gifts are to be a prophet. This is why Ephesians 4:11(NKJV) says, "And he himself gave some to be apostles, some prophets, some evangelists, and some pastors and teachers." Some people may be able to sing, dance, or tap their feet. Others may have concrete faith, but this chapter will discuss prophets and prophetess'.

There are no limitations as several prophets say that *POPPA* said He will rise! The scriptures give no indication who can and can't be a prophet or prophetess. Neither are there as a guide to show how to be a prophet, who to prophesy to, or how much to say. When it is permitted for you to speak, I advise you not to hold back. I believe in speaking things into existence. If utterance cannot be given, then the word won't be in the atmosphere. This a three-fold cord. Without speaking, Satan can't hear the plan of God and attempt to stop them. If there was a life or death situation, not speaking could leave blood on your hands. It is not wise to withhold a blessing or correction when the Father permits it. That is the definition of grieving in the spirit. Personal feelings cannot become attached. If it is meant to be heard then it is mandatory to be spoken. Most people hold back because they are afraid that they may be wrong or have arbitrary information; they may also fear that the person will not accept what they have to say. Don't worry about the other person's reception. That doesn't matter.

Obedience is what is required. Remember that Jesus Christ said it best when he said, "He who receives you receives me, and he who receives me receives him who sent me." (Matthew 10:40). Thus, a person shouldn't reject someone or become angry with them for a prophetic word that is spoken. But wasn't Jesus rejected? The unbelievers and people who doubt or reject the prophet also brings destruction upon themselves (Acts 3:23). The word could be good. When people neglect the word and are not vigilant, then the word will not be accomplished.

Matthew 13:5 (NKJV)
"A prophet is not without honor except in
his own country and in his own house."

It can be hard for family and friends to accept
prophets. They may agree at times, but deep
inside they are doubting. The people of Jesus'
hometown didn't believe He was who He claimed
He was. This same unbelief goes on today. When
Jesus said, "No prophet is accepted in own
country..." (Luke 4:24). He meant the regions
where He roamed. It was difficult at first for His
own mother and Joseph to fathom who He really
was. It is sort of like a person who does something
that surpasses reality. Even though the thing has
come to pass, a person can't foster it in their head.
It's the same phenomenon as a child who grows
up so fast that they are now graduating college. It
can be real, but still unbelievable!

This unbelief causes questions and may have
someone acting ill-mannered towards a prophet.
Ezekiel and Isaiah didn't get discouraged in their
time, and neither should today's prophets. Again,
callings and gifts should not be thrown away.
What God has for you is for you and no one else.
Prophets are birthed every day. Some never grow
into their full potential because they deny the

Spirit or regret it. Some of us are called, but few are chosen. "Before I formed you in the womb I knew you; before you were born I sanctified you, I ordained you in a prophet to the Nations." (Jeremiah 1:5). It is meant for us to be who we are, whether we are a prophet or not. If we run from our purpose then we will have a miserable life. We will end up like Jonah until we come into acceptance. Nothing will go our way and we will always feel a void. Deep down inside, one will always fill the void more they are doing what they are supposed to. Some walk into the fulfillment and others don't. God will continue to call out to us, but will we answer? He knew who we were meant to be before we knew ourselves. He made our destiny before we were born. Surely, if the great Sheppard has counted every single hair on our head and called us His children then He will speak to us, speak through us, and speak of us.

Moses said, "The Lord your God will raise up for you a prophet like ne from your midst, from your brethren. Him you shall hear." (Deuteronomy 18:15) "If the prophet is induced to speak anything I the Lord have induced that prophet" (Ezekial 14:9 NKJV).

II Peter 1:19 (NKJV)
"And so, we have the prophetic word
confirmed, which you
do well to heed as a light that shines
in a dark, place,until the day dawns
and the morning star rises in your hearts.

The key to II Peter 1:19 is confirmed. Confirm has a beautiful meaning when you are unsure about something. To a lot of people, prophets just babble. Their words seem unclear until it is confirmed. Confirmation is the realization, manifestation and evidence of what was said. I have been in a situation where I didn't believe what the prophets had said. I mean, I believed at first because prophet kept saying the same things. Seers that I knew and didn't know spoke of this divine deliverance. When years carried on and it seem like the enemy was winning every battle, I became weary and felt like everything that I heard was a lie, especially when things stopped looking the way they were predicted.

I under-estimated the glory of God. I began to count myself out and the revelations that were foretold I just erased out of my mind. Even though nothing came to pass of what the prophets spoke, I must have believed because it is impossible to please God without faith. If I give up then I have already lost the blessings, whether they were coming or not. I have come this far so why should I give up now. Even if victory appears so far away, I must make the best out of the present time. Defeat shall not overcome me. God is a miraculous God and His timing is not my timing.

Learning to depend solely on the Most High is a challenging task. Therefore, I believe Jesus told Peter that he believed because he saw Jesus; but greater are those who don't see Him but believe. While writing this chapter, I took into perspective everything that I have learn doesn't have to add up. My point of view seems right to me, but is it right to God? Matthew 18:16 says, "By the mouth of two or three witnesses every word shall be established." If many people are telling me the same thing repeatedly, then it must have some truth to it. I recall events where even my own mother said she had seen things in the spiritual realm, and then later it happened. Through recent experiences I believe God is with me. Truthfully, I don't understand what is going on now. I am wrestling between doubt and faith. I will take a hold of the words of the prophets. I have already lost everything, so I have nothing left to lose— only something to gain. Even after words have been spoken to me, I must still seek the Creator for myself. At the end of the day, no mom, dad, prophet, or preacher can live my life; only I can.

It is hard to get a grip on what others say when you believe they are speaking out of the nature of their own heart. So many people have been wrong trying to speak into another person's life. There are ways to tell a true prophet from a false prophet. There are fakes in this world (See Deuteronomy 18:21-22). Not to say that they are intentionally lying, but I have seen where some prophet's revelations come true with most of the people that they speak to. A few revelations were wrong because they were more in tune with God on one person than the other. That doesn't mean that they are false prophets. The case may be that they received it from the flesh and not the spirit.

Don't always discredit or discount a prophet. Everyone is entitled to make mistakes (See I Corinthians 14:29-32). If you read I Corinthians, you will see that Paul made a proclamation that he knew that the spirits of the prophets were subject to the prophets. This meant that there was a probability that they could be wrong, so another seer was there to judge the outcome.

Matthew 12:39
"An evil and adulterous generation
 seeks after a sign,
and no sign will be given to it except the
sign of the prophet Jonah."

In the book of Jonah, Jonah was caught up in his own deliverance. He was not concerned about saving the people in the boat with him. Jonah was a prophet who disobeyed by attempting to run in the opposite direction. When Jesus referred to the sign of Jonah, He was saying that people are selfish, self-centered, self-righteous, and that they want magic to appear before their eyes. The only thing they will see is the life, death, and resurrection of Jesus Christ.

Jonah was in a whale's belly for three days and nights. Jesus was in the grave for the same amount of days. Jesus was letting us know that if we respond to him in due time, then God will be merciful and withhold His punishments from us. The story of Jonah showed us that no matter what we try to do in our own power and will, God's will, will be done.

10 Things That Confirm Your Prophetic Call

Ministry to the church – If you find yourself drawn to ministering to believers, believers who have backslid, or non-believers.

Unique Approach – From the beginning, you have always done things differently. You tend to always surprise others. There is silver lining in this cloud – people will never forget you!

Swinging the pendulum – Prophets are notorious for swinging wildly from one extreme to the next. However, the Lord is gracious and does not leave His prophet in a pity party. He will always pull you out of those times.

Humiliation – Jesus himself was stripped and laid bare on the cross. He was humiliated before everyone, and you too must go through the same experience many times.

Singleness of Purpose – There is no compromise with a prophet. You are saved or you are not. You are anointed or you are not. You are chosen or you are not. There is no shade of grey, only black and white. Hot or cold is acceptable, but lukewarm is not!

Unconscious revelation – Flowing in the Spirit without realizing it. It is sensing whether something is right or wrong, flowing in dreams and visions, seeing things from God's perspective in the Spirit.

Allegorical thinking – Seeing deeper meanings and bigger pictures that others don't see; you often use parables to minister.

Prayer orientation – You love to pray and seek God on behalf of yourself and others,

Bringing God's presence through music – Prophets have an anointing from God that releases His presence in praise and worship. That worship includes dancing, singing, or simply worshipping God with all their might. This is not talent, this is an anointing!

Tough experiences in life – There are times when a prophet can feel just like John the Baptist. You can feel stuck in the wilderness and misunderstood, but the time does come to be who you are called to be in the world. Tough experiences help shape the calling on their lives.

Chapter 19

Mercy

I Chronicles 16:34 (NKJV)

"Oh, give thanks to the Lord, for he is good! For his mercy endures forever."

You are not lucky. It is mercy. Mercy is when you have been spared for all that you have done wrong. Mercy is when you deserve to be punished, but you don't receive the punishment or the consequences to your actions. It is like when you are guilty of a crime, but get exonerated. Mercy is when you do drugs, alcohol, don't eat properly, or work out, but you are still in good health. It is when your kids are safe and your spouse is protected. A lot of us have the wrong idea of mercy, so we don't realize it when it's happening. We say it's good luck or a coincidence. We downplay mercy so we don't value it. In this corrupt world, many things are under-valued and taken for granted. Some of us can be ungrateful when infliction is bestowed upon us and unthankful when it is taken away. God sends forth His mercies and truth so we can see His hand amid a storm, but most still deny the effect. If we can't see it carnally then we doubt the source thereof. This is why Jesus Christ said better are they that don't see, but believe.

Romans 9:18 (NKJV)
"Therefore, He has mercy on whom He wills, and whom He wills He hardens."

A lot of people don't believe in the strength of mercy because they say that God should have done that. In my opinion, they are attempting to think for God. Perhaps they are delusional that they are the Maker or God is the craft. However, just like a CEO of a company decides on who he or she may give a promotion to, God is able to raise up whom He pleases or allow them to remain stagnant. Many of us have been depressed or anxious because of God's merciless mechanisms.

I for one have warred with myself if the presence of a creator even existed. I said to myself that if there is a God, maybe I am serving the wrong one because my life is a complete mess. I wake up every morning like I am already living in hell. David fought one giant Goliath, but it's like I'm up against six of them. Daniel's prophecy was only withheld from him for three weeks, but mine has been kept away for years. Paul killed the children of Israel, I've murdered no one, but I've been convicted and treated as such. Jesus Christ was in the fire with the three Hebrew boys, and it's like I'm in the furnace alone while the fire has been turned up ten times hotter. When I try to be humble like God, a rumble comes my way. I know that I am not perfect. I never claimed to be a saint, but I do pray for mercy. Even Jesus Christ Himself pleaded for mercy (see Matthew 26:39).

Our heavenly Father did not spare His own son. There are some of us He will not be lenient on. This does not necessarily mean that we have done wrong or evil. God may not be soft-hearted on us simply because it is not His will. The script was already written before we were born. We have to acknowledge that the creator sees further down the line than we could ever imagine.

I should be honest; I know what it feels like to have all hope lost. Many people say that we should be happy because we are alive, and we have all our five senses. What about those who lack some of their senses? What encouragement do you have for people who are not in their right mind? I have been at a point in my life where I felt that death was better than life. I wanted to die because my problems overwhelmed me. I felt that God was not merciful. I believed in my heart that I was abandoned and destroyed. The covenant that was sworn to me was forgotten as far as I could see (Deuteronomy 4:31).

I had to remind myself time after time that maybe it's just not my time to shine. Days seemed far away, but I had to persevere to make it to that appointed date. I was raised to assume that God was very compassionate and merciful (James 5:11). I remember the psalmist saying, "I have been young and now I am old; yet, I have not seen the righteous forsaken, nor his descendants begging bread. He is ever merciful and lends; and his descendents are blessed." (Psalm 37:25-26) I remember the scripture saying, "The Lord is good; His mercy endures to all generations." (Psalm 100:5)

So I asked myself was it a contradiction for David to speak so confidently and then ask himself if His mercy has ceased forever. Has His promises failed evermore? Has God forgotten to be gracious? Has He in anger shut up His tender mercies? (Psalm 77:8-9) I figured out that to be sure of the events and occurrences surrounding our lives, we have to backtrack our steps and remember the times that we have been touched by His mercy before. We have to recall the previous victories and all the times that we wiggled away from the penalties that we earned, whether it was of the exoneration or not. God abdicates ramifications and ambivalence.

Even when we are sinners, God extricates and forgives us (see Hebrews 8:12).

Matthew 5:7
"Blessed are the merciful, for they shall obtain mercy."
God's mercy is set upon those who fear Him. Some people get the wrong idea when it says to *fear* God. God doesn't want us to be afraid of Him. He wants us to love Him unconditionally. When it says fear the Lord in the scriptures, fear means to respect. Respect is different from being frightened. When we respect someone, we honor what they stand for. Even if we don't always agree with them, we are still considerate of their intentions. To fear God is to respect His word, thoughts, and actions. To fear God is to trust and be confident in the outcome. When

we displease God then we disrespect Him and deserve to be punished (See Exodus 20:3-6). God let it be known that He will forgive transgression and iniquity but by no means clear the guilty (Numbers 14:18). People have the tendency to want mercy but not want to give mercy. They remind me of the servant whom his master forgave his debt, but when the servant saw someone that owed him less money than what he owed his master, he beat the man that owed him and threw him in prison.

To obtain mercy, we must write it on the tablet of our heart and bind it around our neck.

For mercy is on those who fear the Most High. Why should we expect to be saved or delivered when we won't relieve the next person?

If you've ever heard of quid pro quo, then you know what I am talking about. A fair exchange is not robbery. One hand is supposed to help the other. When you think about it, mercy is a remarkable thing. Mercy triumphs over judgment (James 2:13). No matter what people may say or do, when it comes to mercy we have favor. Prostitutes, rapists, murderers, thieves, liars. And fornicators can go to heaven because of mercy. As a matter of fact, God prefers mercy, not sacrifice (Hosea 6:6).

Chapter 20

Grace

Grace is a wonderful thing when you fall under it. It is the stride in your movement. A lot of people don't know the difference between mercy and grace. This chapter should shine a light on the meanings.

G – God's
R – Righteousness
A – At
C – Christ's
E – Expense

By one man named Adam, death came upon mankind. By another man named Jesus, life more abundantly was provided. By one man named Moses, the law of the land was given. Through another man named Jesus, grace and truth came about (Luke 1:17). What exactly is grace? It sounds good to most people. The above acronym is an effortless way to define grace. It really is

God's righteousness at Christ's expense. God grew angry with the world in Noah's days that He wiped out millions of people. He again became indignant by the two cities and obliterated Sodom and Gomorrah. Still, the people on earth sinned and offered up sacrifices, which was the blood of many different animals. So many animals were executed without a change of heart. The offering up of bulls and goats was not enough for the Most High any more. A price had to be paid for human penalties.

Fortunately, that expense was liable at the death of Christ. Therefore, God doesn't see us all as corrupt and sinful creatures. He views us through the blood of His only son, which in return makes us spotless. It is something like looking at a movie through 3D glasses or seeing a dirty person that is covered with clean clothes. Perhaps you knew someone that wanted to harm a person but they didn't do it because they knew that person's family. Grace and mercy are almost similar. They are not the same. Mercy is when you are being spared. Grace is when you are being blessed beyond what you deserve.

A wise man once said that if someone places a clean cup in front of you, then place a dirty cup in front of you, no one should have to tell you which cup to drink out of. So, I say to you after I finish this chapter, no one should have to tell you what to choose.

Exodus 33:19
"I will be gracious to whom I will be gracious, and I will have compassion on whom I will have compassion"

I recall reading the story of two famous brothers. In the story, Jacob told Esau "Please take my blessing that is brought to you, because God has dealt with me, and because I have enough." (Genesis 33:11). The key word in the scripture is the word "enough". When we please God, we will be granted with measurements above our measure. God wants His children to enjoy life on earth. He wants us to have nice cars, houses, clothes, and beautiful spouses. Look at how Job, Abraham, and Isaac lived. If you don't think that the redeemer wants us to have fine things then search the scriptures of Adam and Eve. Even when they disobeyed God's word and found out that they were naked, God took the clothes made of leaves from them and replaced them with garments of fur (Genesis 3:21). He didn't want them itching and getting scratched by leaves, so he gave them tunics of skin so they could be comfortable. **However, our King does not let anyone fall under grace. We should be in line like Abel and not get declined like Cain did.** We have to be accepted. The ancient days told Moses, "For you have found grace in my sight, and I know you by name (Exodus 33:17)." Therefore, it is good to say that we must ingratiate.

To find grace in one's sight is to have favor. When we have grace for God, then He moves on our behalf. Grace is a wonderful and intimate feeling; there is so much that it is nearly indescribable, so one must encounter it. Grace is knowledge and the sudden movement of comfort and joy. It is when you are amid a storm and you are still at peace. It is like when God said unto Paul, "My grace is sufficient for you, for my strength is made perfect in weakness." (II Corinthians 12:19) When we can't go on anymore Grace kicks in.

Galatians 5:4 (NKJV)
"You have become estranged from Christ, you who attempt to be justified by law; you have fallen from grace."

A woman once told me that I was planning something big (which I was). She told me not to do it because it will get in the way of Yahweh's Grace. Sometimes, we get in our own way. We may believe we are perfecting a thing but we are hindering or stopping a miracle. If we do things on our own all the time we will grow arrogant, stubborn, and believe we don't need the assistance of the Light. If only we all knew that our Lord is a sun and shield; the Lord will give grace and glory. No good thing will He withholds from those who walk uprightly (Psalm 84:11).

When we try to work at it out alone or through the ways of the world, then we have fallen from grace. It is only through grace that we are saved through faith. It is a gift, not of works so that we will not boast (Ephesians 2:8).

It is okay to be a hard worker as well as provide for yourself and your family, but when you start to think that it is all about the works or the law of the land, then remind yourself that it is written, "If by grace, then it is no longer of works; otherwise grace is no longer grace. But if it is of works it is no longer grace, otherwise work is no longer work." (Romans 11:6) Do let grace be poured upon you forever with all wisdom, and produce so that through Christ's blood one can receive forgiveness of sins according to the riches of grace. (Ephesians 1:7)

Outro

Mostly everything that is not fully explained throughout the contents of this book will be elaborated more in Volume II. Volume II of the Inner Voice is somewhat like a sequel or series that elucidates my findings. The name of the sequel is Belly of the Beast. It has been once said that my teachings are like that of a college professor. The students have never been introduced to me, and they know little about the subject I am teaching. However, while I explain the theories, application, and principles of the matter, the students will be in awe because they will sense that I know a lot about my calling. However, just as they are about to gain understanding of my teachings, I will grab an eraser and erase all the writings from the board. They may become more confused than they were originally. It is different not knowing something and finally getting a taste of what of knowledge. Yet, some are unable to grasp or comprehend the knowledge in its entirety.

"Belly of the Beast" will be more of the board for you to read. Nevertheless, I must remind you that I am only a planter. I plant the seeds while someone else may come and water them. But it is God that gives you the increase, meaning I am only here to start the growing process of your wisdom and knowledge of these finding. Someone else may come along to water you, keep you fresh, and cultivate your growing process. However, it is God that opens your heart and mind to give you full understanding. It is God who turns a mustard seed to the biggest tree in the world. Now, when your growing process starts is completely up to God. It may take days before you grasp all that was implemented. It may take months, years, or even decades. Believe it or not, some people may never learn. It is not meant for every seed to flourish. The best thing I can advise for you to do is pray to your Creator for maturity and lean not to your own understanding.

Until next time, may peace be unto you.

About the Author

RAHSAAN AKI TAYLOR is an innocent man that has been wrongly convicted of a capital murder that occurred on Halloween night in 2007. He was framed by two perpetrators who happened to be brother and sister. The judge presiding over Rahsaan's case accepted false testimonies against him. The judge knowingly stated in his records that he is aware of the perjury, but still allowed it. Medical experts were not allowed by the court because it would have proven Rahsaan's innocence. However, lies and deals were setup between the prosecutors and a witness within the face of the public. Furthermore, several officers detained a suggestive and illegal photo into evidence. Instead of a constitutional photo array, they placed one single photo to be chosen. With the ineffective assistance of counsels and the injustice of appeals, Rahsaan has yet to prevail. If you have any information that will help or if you are willing to assist in any way, please feel free to contact:

Justice for Rahsaan Foundation
PO Box 193302
Little Rock, AR 72219
(501) 541-9279

References

"Theory." Merriam-Webster. Merriam-Webster, n.d.
Web. 14 Apr. 2017. <https://www.merriam-webster.
com/dictionary/theory>.

"Faith." Merriam-Webster. Merriam-Webster, n.d. Web.
14 Apr. 2017. <https://www.merriam-webster.com/
dictionary/faith>.

Perception dictionary definition | perception
defined. N.p., n.d. Web. 14 Apr. 2017. <http://www.
yourdictionary.com/perception>.

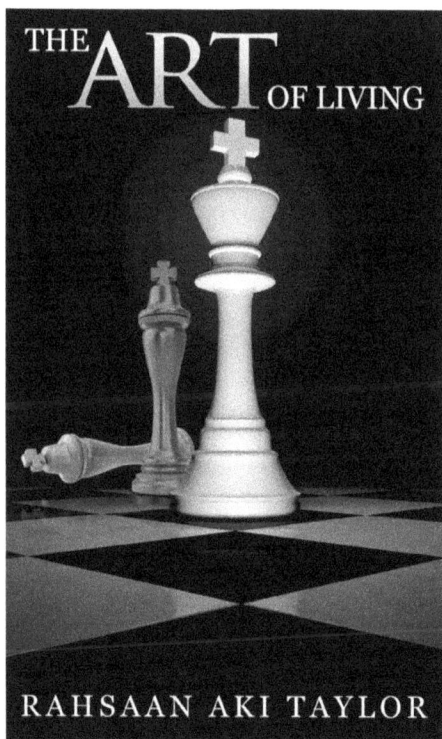

Also Available from
J. Kenkade Publishing

Women & Girls Breaking Free from Statistics & Strongholds

DIVAS Unchained

NIOKA SMITH, M.Ed.

ISBN: 978-1-944486-01-3
Visit www.divasunchained.com

A powerful, chain-breaking truth of the spiritual and emotional struggles of women & girls. DIVAS Unchained exposes Satan's lies and empowers women and girls with the tools to break away from the tangled chains of strongholds into the unraveled embrace of God's love and purpose for their lives.

Also Available from
J. Kenkade Publishing

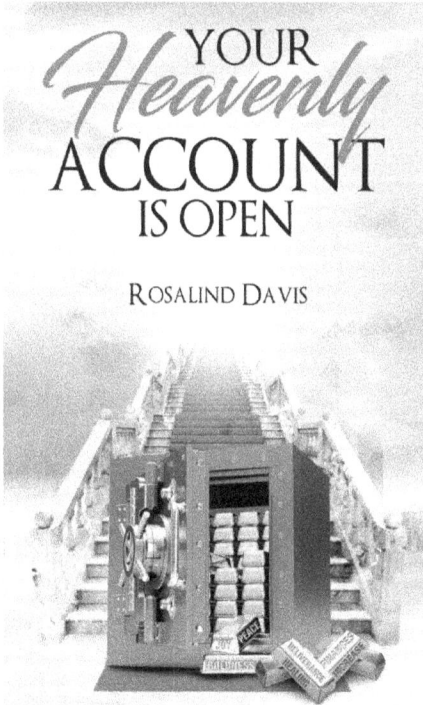

ISBN: 978-1-944486-00-6
Visit www.jkenkade.com

The author shares her personal encounter with God in which
He revealed to her a Heavenly Account that is available to
all of His children. This devotional will help you discover
the process of making deposits and receiving withdrawals
from your own personal Heavenly Account.

www.ingramcontent.com/pod-product-compliance
Lightning Source LLC
LaVergne TN
LVHW011324080426
835513LV00006B/182